LET'S LEARN

GERMAN
PICTURE DICTIONARY

By
The Editors of
Passport Books

Illustrated by
Marlene Goodman

PASSPORT BOOKS
a division of *NTC Publishing Group*
Lincolnwood, Illinois USA

Welcome to the *Let's Learn German* Picture Dictionary!

Here's an exciting way for you to learn more than 1,500 German words that will help you speak about many of your favorite subjects. With these words, you will be able to talk in German about your house, sports, outer space, the ocean, and many more subjects.

This dictionary is fun to use. On each page, you will see drawings with the German and English words that describe them underneath. These drawings are usually part of a large, colorful scene. See if you can find all the words in the big scene and then try to remember how to say each one in German. You will enjoy looking at the pictures more and more as you learn more German.

You will notice that almost all the German words in this book have **der, die,** or **das** before them. These words simply mean "the" and are usually used when you talk about things in German.

At the back of the book, you will find a German-English Glossary and Index and an English-German Glossary and Index, where you can look up words in alphabetical order, and find out exactly where the words are located in the dictionary. There is also a section that explains how you say German sounds as well as pronunciation guides that will help you say each German word correctly.

This is a book you can look at over and over again, and each time you look, you will find something new. You'll learn the German words for people, places, and things you know, and you may even learn some new words in English as you go along!

Illustrations by Terrie Meider
7. Clothing; 15. People in our Community; 18. Sports; 28. Colors; 29. The Family Tree; 30. Shapes; 31. Numbers; 32. Map of the World.

1995 Printing

Table of Contents
Inhaltsverzeichnis

1. Our Classroom   Unser Klassenzimmer

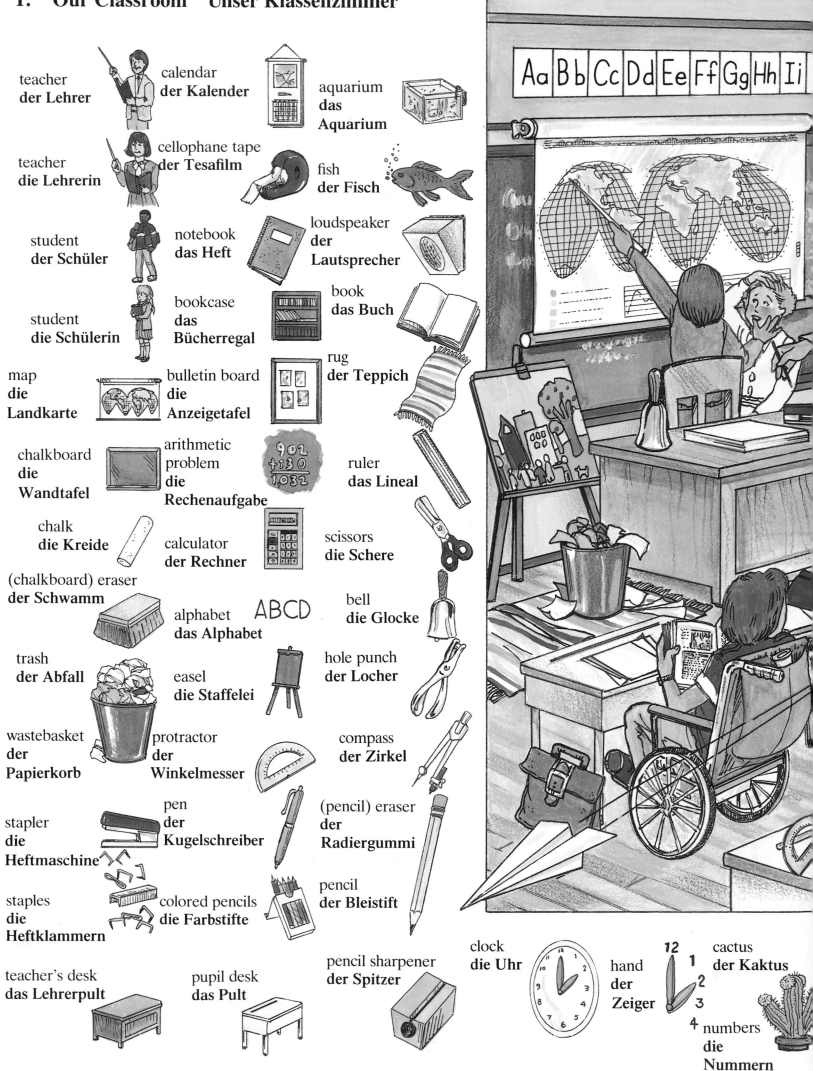

teacher
der Lehrer

teacher
die Lehrerin

student
der Schüler

student
die Schülerin

map
die Landkarte

chalkboard
die Wandtafel

chalk
die Kreide

(chalkboard) eraser
der Schwamm

trash
der Abfall

wastebasket
der Papierkorb

stapler
die Heftmaschine

staples
die Heftklammern

teacher's desk
das Lehrerpult

calendar
der Kalender

cellophane tape
der Tesafilm

notebook
das Heft

bookcase
das Bücherregal

bulletin board
die Anzeigetafel

arithmetic problem
die Rechenaufgabe

calculator
der Rechner

alphabet
das Alphabet

easel
die Staffelei

protractor
der Winkelmesser

pen
der Kugelschreiber

colored pencils
die Farbstifte

pupil desk
das Pult

aquarium
das Aquarium

fish
der Fisch

loudspeaker
der Lautsprecher

book
das Buch

rug
der Teppich

ruler
das Lineal

scissors
die Schere

bell
die Glocke

hole punch
der Locher

compass
der Zirkel

(pencil) eraser
der Radiergummi

pencil
der Bleistift

pencil sharpener
der Spitzer

clock
die Uhr

hand
der Zeiger

cactus
der Kaktus

numbers
die Nummern

plant
die Pflanze

glue
der Klebstoff

globe
der Globus

picture
das Bild

paint
die Farbe

paintbrush
der Pinsel

paper
das Papier

crayon
der Buntstift

2. Our House

Unser Haus

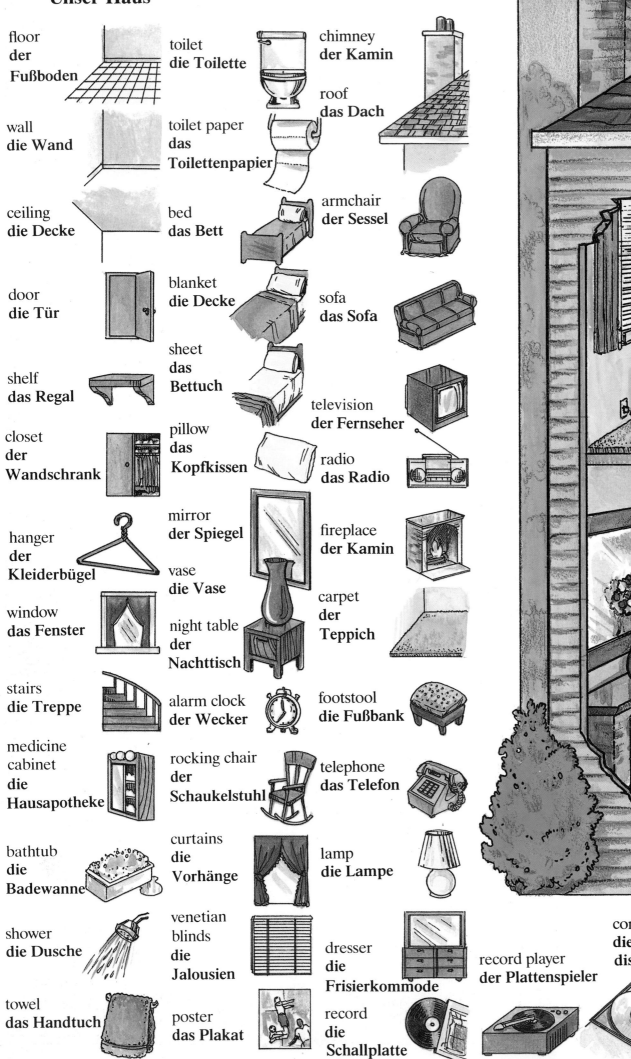

floor
der Fußboden

wall
die Wand

ceiling
die Decke

door
die Tür

shelf
das Regal

closet
der Wandschrank

hanger
der Kleiderbügel

window
das Fenster

stairs
die Treppe

medicine cabinet
die Hausapotheke

bathtub
die Badewanne

shower
die Dusche

towel
das Handtuch

toilet
die Toilette

toilet paper
das Toilettenpapier

bed
das Bett

blanket
die Decke

sheet
das Bettuch

pillow
das Kopfkissen

mirror
der Spiegel

vase
die Vase

night table
der Nachttisch

alarm clock
der Wecker

rocking chair
der Schaukelstuhl

curtains
die Vorhänge

venetian blinds
die Jalousien

poster
das Plakat

chimney
der Kamin

roof
das Dach

armchair
der Sessel

sofa
das Sofa

television
der Fernseher

radio
das Radio

fireplace
der Kamin

carpet
der Teppich

footstool
die Fußbank

telephone
das Telefon

lamp
die Lampe

dresser
die Frisierkommode

record
die Schallplatte

compact disc
die Compact disc

record player
der Plattenspieler

videocassette player
der Videorecorder

cassette tape
die Kassette

cassette player
der
Kassettenrecorder

bedroom
das
Schlafzimmer

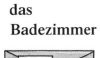
bathroom
das
Badezimmer

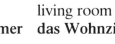
living room
das Wohnzimmer

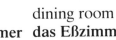
dining room
das Eßzimmer

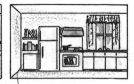
kitchen
die Küche

3. The Kitchen
die Küche

| counter **die Theke** | oven **der Backofen** | faucet **der Wasserhahn** | pan **die Pfanne** | paper towels **die Papiertücher** | chair **der Stuhl** |

| table **der Tisch** | refrigerator **der Kühlschrank** | dishwasher **die Spülmaschine** | electric mixer **der Mixer** | ice cubes **die Eiswürfel** | apron **die Schürze** |

| microwave oven **der Mikrowellenherd** | freezer **die Tiefkühltruhe** | food processor **die Küchenmaschine** | drawer **die Schublade** | spatula **die Spachtel** | flour **das Mehl** |

| stove **der Herd** | sink **das Spülbecken** | kettle **der Wasserkessel** | toaster **der Toaster** | dishes **das Geschirr** | sponge **der Schwamm** |

The Utility Room
der Abstellraum

washing machine
die Waschmaschine

iron
das Bügeleisen

screw
die Schraube

toolbox
der Werkzeugkasten

laundry detergent
das Waschmittel

laundry
die Wäsche

broom
der Besen

mop
der Mop

screwdriver
der Schraubenzieher

wrench
der Schraubenschlüssel

wood
das Holz

board
das Brett

vacuum cleaner
der Staubsauger

dustpan
die Kehrichtschaufel

drill
der Bohrer

electrical outlet
die Steckdose

sandpaper
das Sandpapier

flashlight
die Taschenlampe

hammer
der Hammer

brick
der Backstein

ironing board
das Bügelbrett

nail
der Nagel

file
die Feile

tape measure
das Bandmaß

saw
die Säge

clothes dryer
der Trockner

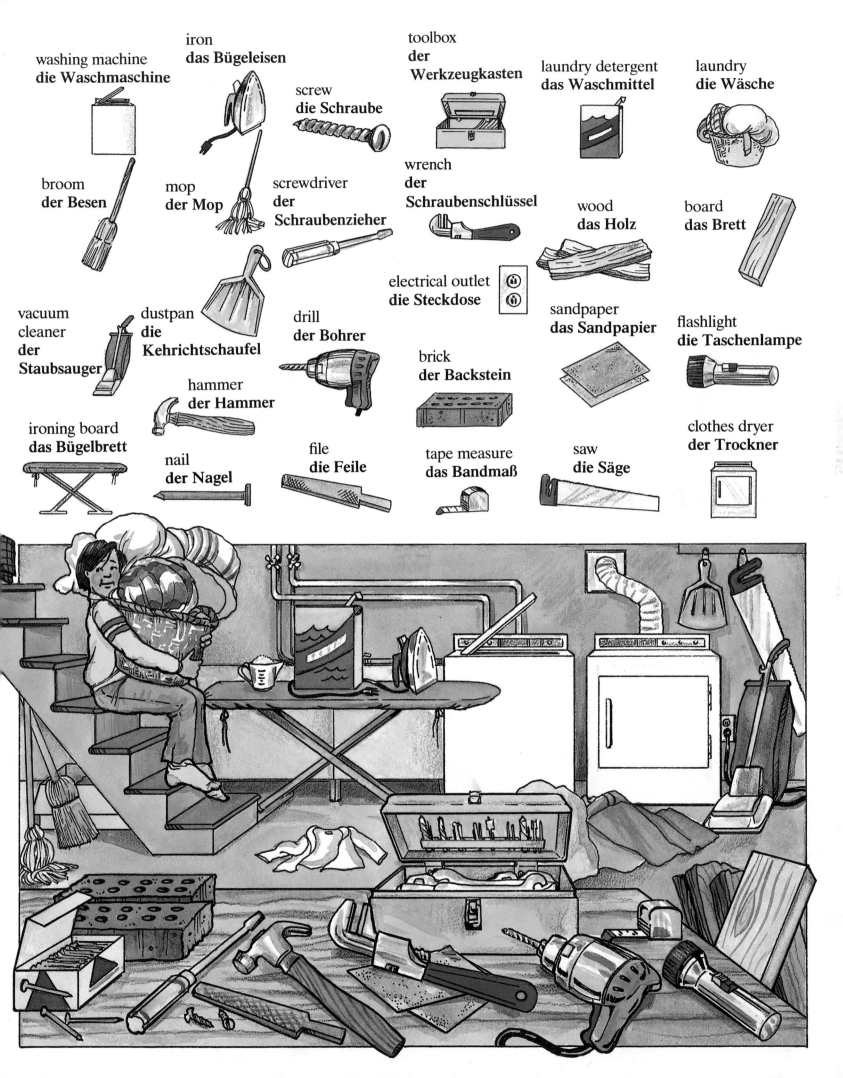

4. The Attic
die Dachstube

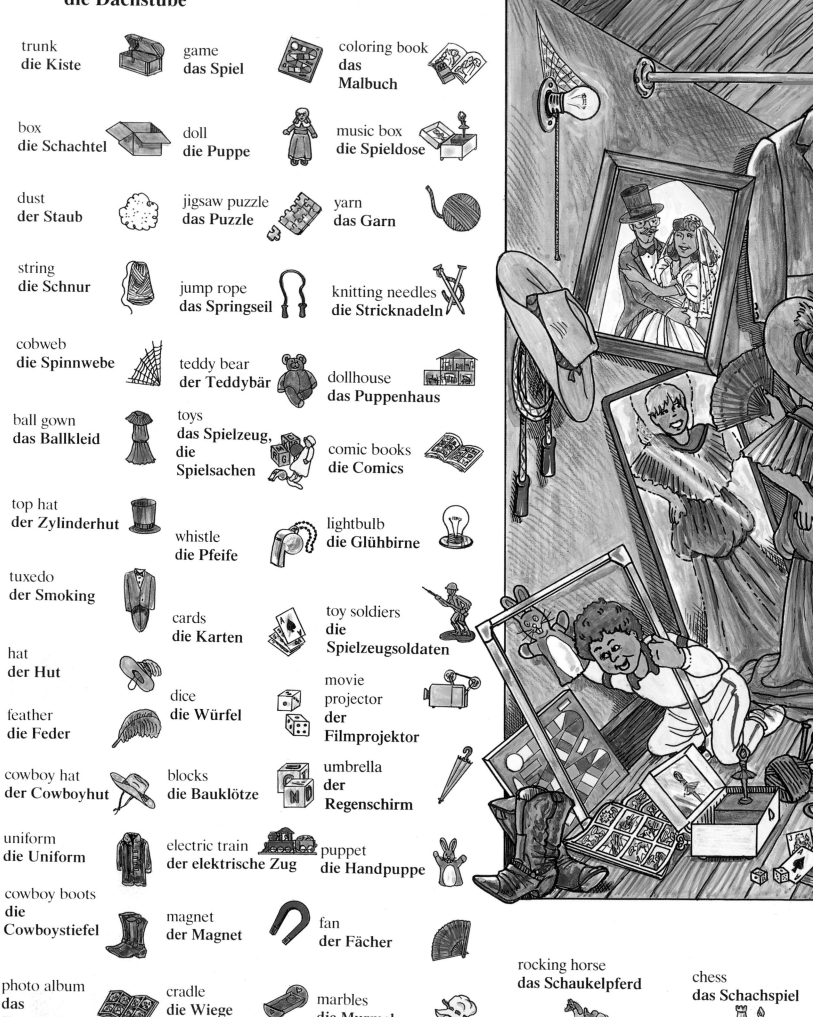

trunk
die Kiste

game
das Spiel

coloring book
das Malbuch

box
die Schachtel

doll
die Puppe

music box
die Spieldose

dust
der Staub

jigsaw puzzle
das Puzzle

yarn
das Garn

string
die Schnur

jump rope
das Springseil

knitting needles
die Stricknadeln

cobweb
die Spinnwebe

teddy bear
der Teddybär

dollhouse
das Puppenhaus

ball gown
das Ballkleid

toys
**das Spielzeug,
die Spielsachen**

comic books
die Comics

top hat
der Zylinderhut

whistle
die Pfeife

lightbulb
die Glühbirne

tuxedo
der Smoking

cards
die Karten

toy soldiers
die Spielzeugsoldaten

hat
der Hut

dice
die Würfel

movie projector
der Filmprojektor

feather
die Feder

cowboy hat
der Cowboyhut

blocks
die Bauklötze

umbrella
der Regenschirm

uniform
die Uniform

electric train
der elektrische Zug

puppet
die Handpuppe

cowboy boots
die Cowboystiefel

magnet
der Magnet

fan
der Fächer

photo album
das Fotoalbum

cradle
die Wiege

marbles
die Murmeln

rocking horse
das Schaukelpferd

chess
das Schachspiel

photograph **die Photographie**	spinning wheel **das Spinnrad**	picture frame **der Bilderrahmen**	rocking chair **der Schaukelstuhl**	checkers **das Mühlespiel**

5. The Four Seasons (Weather)
die vier Jahreszeiten (das Wetter)

Winter
der Winter

snow
der Schnee

sled
der Schlitten

ice
das Eis

snowplow
der Schneepflug

snowflake
die Schneeflocke

snowmobile
das Schneemobil

icicle
der Eiszapfen

snowman
der Schneemann

shovel
die Schaufel

snowball
der Schneeball

snowstorm
der Schneesturm

log
der Holzklotz

Spring
der Frühling

rain
der Regen

flowers
die Blumen

rainbow
der Regenbogen

flowerbed
das Blumenbeet

stem
der Stengel

petal
das Blütenblatt

bird
der Vogel

vegetable garden
der Gemüsegarten

worm
der Wurm

raindrop
der Regentropfen

lightning
der Blitz

Summer
der Sommer

butterfly
der Schmetterling

fly
die Fliege

fly swatter
die Fliegenklatsche

fan
der Ventilator

sprinkler
der Rasensprenger

grasshopper
die Heuschrecke

lawn mower
der Rasenmäher

barbecue
der Grill

hammock
die Hängematte

yard
der Hof

deck
die Veranda

garden hose
der Gartenschlauch

matches
die Streichhölzer

Fall
der Herbst

wind
der Wind

leaf
das Blatt

branch
der Zweig

fog
der Nebel

rake
der Rechen

clouds
die Wolken

kite
der Drachen

puddle
die Pfütze

mud
der Matsch

bird's nest
das Vogelnest

bush
der Busch

6. At the Supermarket   Im Supermarkt

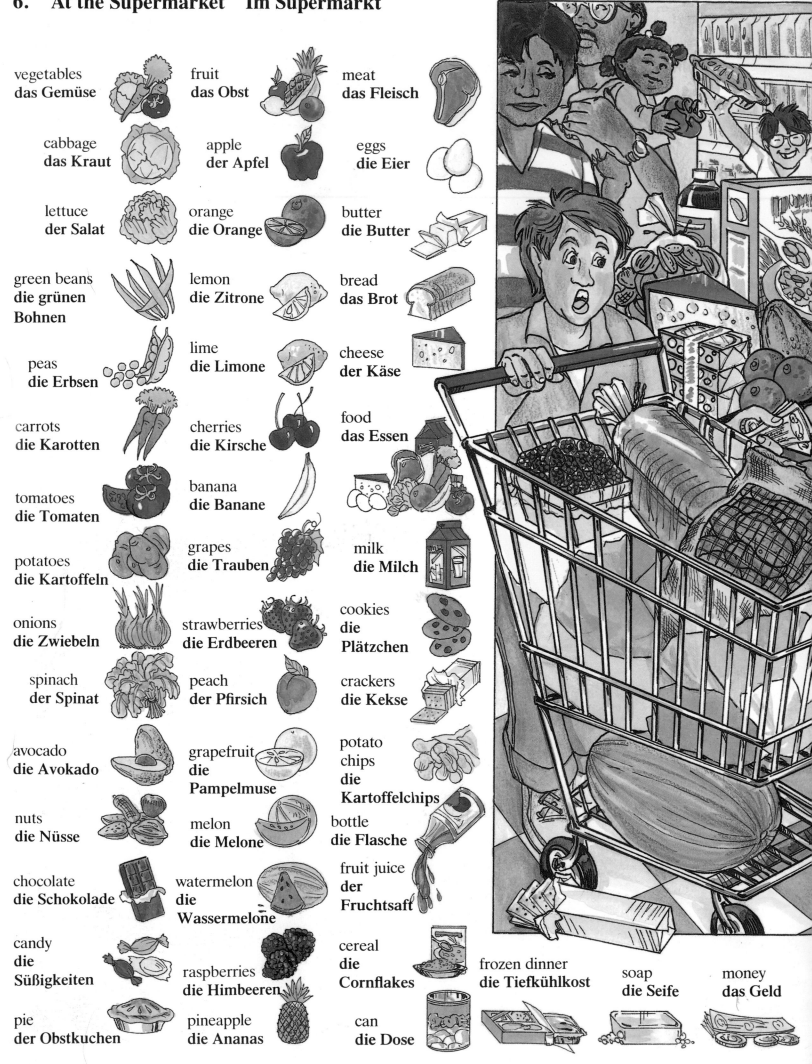

vegetables
das Gemüse

fruit
das Obst

meat
das Fleisch

cabbage
das Kraut

apple
der Apfel

eggs
die Eier

lettuce
der Salat

orange
die Orange

butter
die Butter

green beans
die grünen Bohnen

lemon
die Zitrone

bread
das Brot

peas
die Erbsen

lime
die Limone

cheese
der Käse

carrots
die Karotten

cherries
die Kirsche

food
das Essen

tomatoes
die Tomaten

banana
die Banane

potatoes
die Kartoffeln

grapes
die Trauben

milk
die Milch

onions
die Zwiebeln

strawberries
die Erdbeeren

cookies
die Plätzchen

spinach
der Spinat

peach
der Pfirsich

crackers
die Kekse

avocado
die Avokado

grapefruit
die Pampelmuse

potato chips
die Kartoffelchips

nuts
die Nüsse

melon
die Melone

bottle
die Flasche

chocolate
die Schokolade

watermelon
die Wassermelone

fruit juice
der Fruchtsaft

candy
die Süßigkeiten

raspberries
die Himbeeren

cereal
die Cornflakes

frozen dinner
die Tiefkühlkost

soap
die Seife

money
das Geld

pie
der Obstkuchen

pineapple
die Ananas

can
die Dose

shopping cart
der einen
Einkaufswagen

shopping
bag
die Tüte

sign
das Zeichen

scale
die Waage

price
der Preis

cash register
die Kasse

cashier
die Kassiererin

7. Clothing   Die Kleidung

glasses
die Brille

buckle
die Schnalle

belt
der Gürtel

pants
die Hosen

underwear
die Unterwäsche

collar
der Kragen

blouse
die Bluse

bracelet
das Armband

ring
der Ring

skirt
der Rock

socks
die Socken

shoes
die Schuhe

tie
die Krawatte

sleeve
der Ärmel

suit
der Anzug

shirt
das Hemd

necklace
die Halskette

dress
das Kleid

bathing suit
der Badeanzug

button
der Knopf

earmuffs
die Ohrenschützer

gloves
die Handschuhe

shoelace
der Schnürsenkel

coat
der Mantel

handkerchief
das Taschentuch

sweater
der Pullover

gym shoes
die Turnschuhe

tights
die Strumpfhose

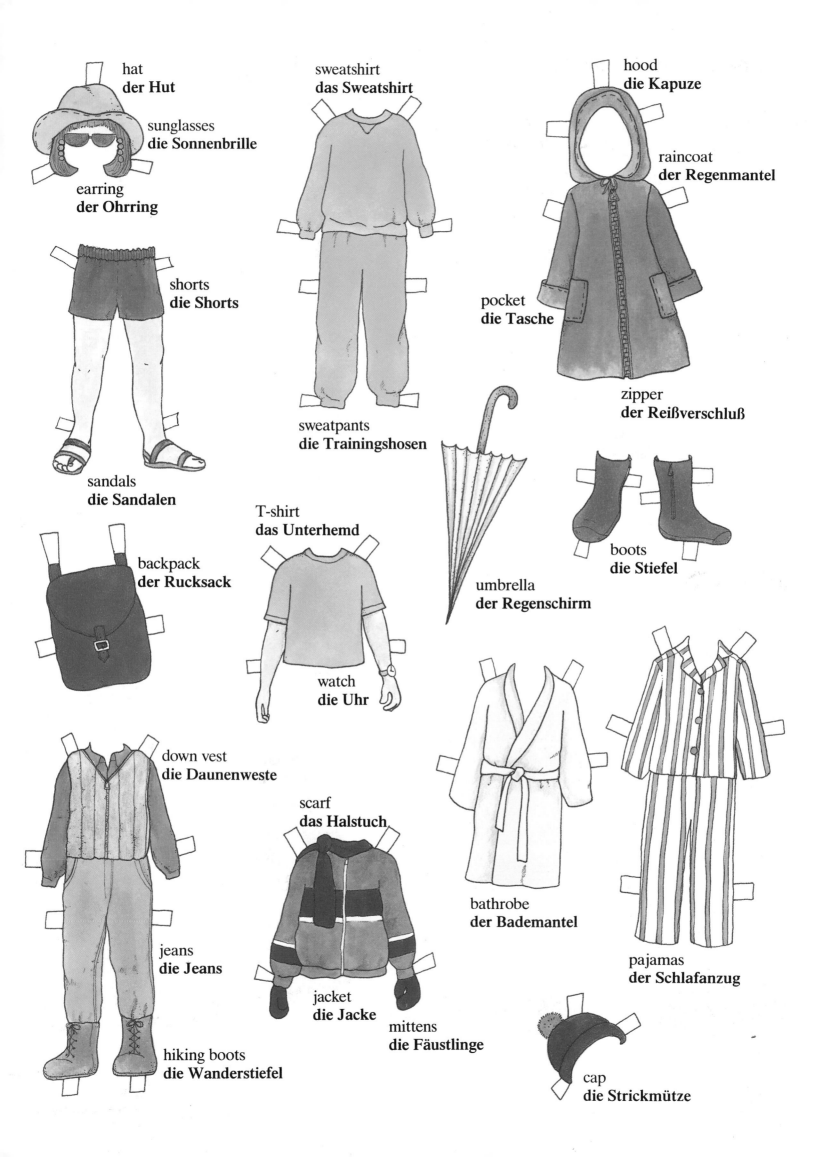

hat
der Hut

sunglasses
die Sonnenbrille

earring
der Ohrring

sweatshirt
das Sweatshirt

hood
die Kapuze

raincoat
der Regenmantel

shorts
die Shorts

pocket
die Tasche

zipper
der Reißverschluß

sweatpants
die Trainingshosen

sandals
die Sandalen

boots
die Stiefel

T-shirt
das Unterhemd

backpack
der Rucksack

umbrella
der Regenschirm

watch
die Uhr

down vest
die Daunenweste

scarf
das Halstuch

bathrobe
der Bademantel

pajamas
der Schlafanzug

jeans
die Jeans

jacket
die Jacke

mittens
die Fäustlinge

hiking boots
die Wanderstiefel

cap
die Strickmütze

8. In the City   In der Stadt

building
das Gebäude

apartment building
das Wohnhaus

train station
der Bahnhof

skyscraper
der Wolkenkratzer

fire escape
die Rettungsleiter

church
die Kirche

factory
die Fabrik

balcony
der Balkon

school
die Schule

smokestack
der Schornstein

fire station
die Feuerwehrzentrale

museum
das Museum

traffic lights
die Verkehrsampel

police station
die Polizeiwache

hospital
das Krankenhaus

manhole cover
der Kanaldeckel

jail
das Gefängnis

drugstore (pharmacy)
die Apotheke

driveway
die Auffahrt

bookstore
die Buchhandlung

movie theater
das Kino

parking lot
der Parkplatz

toy store
der Spielwarenladen

restaurant
das Restaurant

parking meter
die Parkuhr

grocery store
das Lebens– mittelgeschäft

clothing store
der Bekleidungsladen

corner
die Ecke

bakery
die Bäckerei

fire hydrant
der Hydrant

butcher shop
die Metzgerei

hotel
das Hotel

square
der Platz

fountain
der Brunnen

traffic jam
der Verkehrsstau

statue
die Statue

newspaper
die Zeitung

crane
der Kran

bench
die Bank

sign
das Zeichen

playground
der Spielplatz

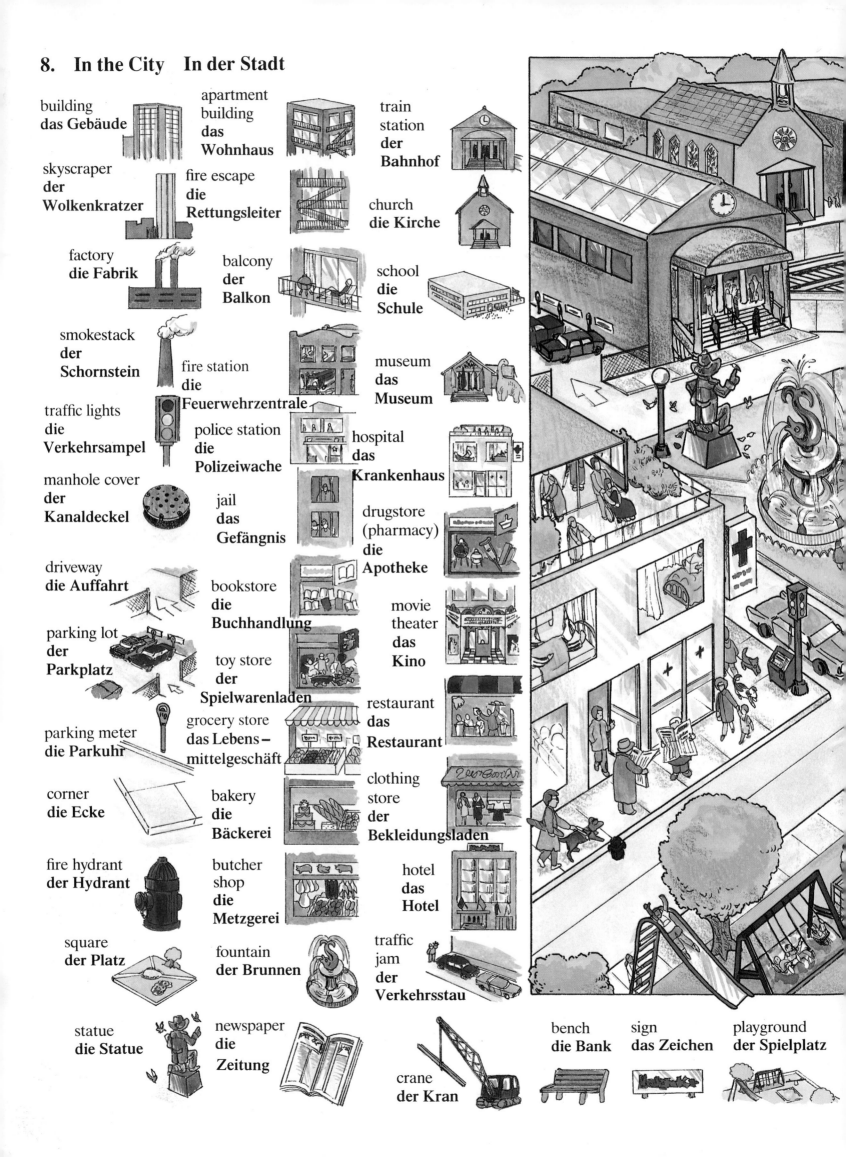

park **der Park** 	jungle gym **das Spielgerät**	swings **die Schaukel** 	

seesaw **die Wippe**	slide **die Rutschbahn**	

sandbox **der Sandkasten**	beach **der Strand** 

9. In the Country   Auf dem Land

farmer
der Bauer

tractor
der Traktor

barn
die Scheune

hay
das Heu

dog
der Hund

puppy
das Hündchen

cat
die Katze

kitten
das Kätzchen

rooster
der Hahn

hen
das Huhn

chick
das Hühnchen

pig
das Schwein

piglet
das Ferkel

rabbit
der Hase

bull
der Bulle

cow
die Kuh

calf
das Kalb

horse
das Pferd

colt
das Fohlen

duck
die Ente

duckling
das Entchen

goat
die Ziege

kid
das Zicklein

goose
die Gans

gosling
das Gänslein

lamb
das Lamm

sheep
das Schaf

mouse
die Maus

horns
die Hörner

donkey
der Esel

bees
die Bienen

frog
der Frosch

pond
der Teich

grass
das Gras

fence
der Zaun

tree
der Baum

shadow
der Schatten

hill
der Hügel

road
der Weg

smoke
der Rauch

picnic
das Picknick

ant
die Ameise

dirt
der Schmutz

tent
das Zelt

sky
der Himmel

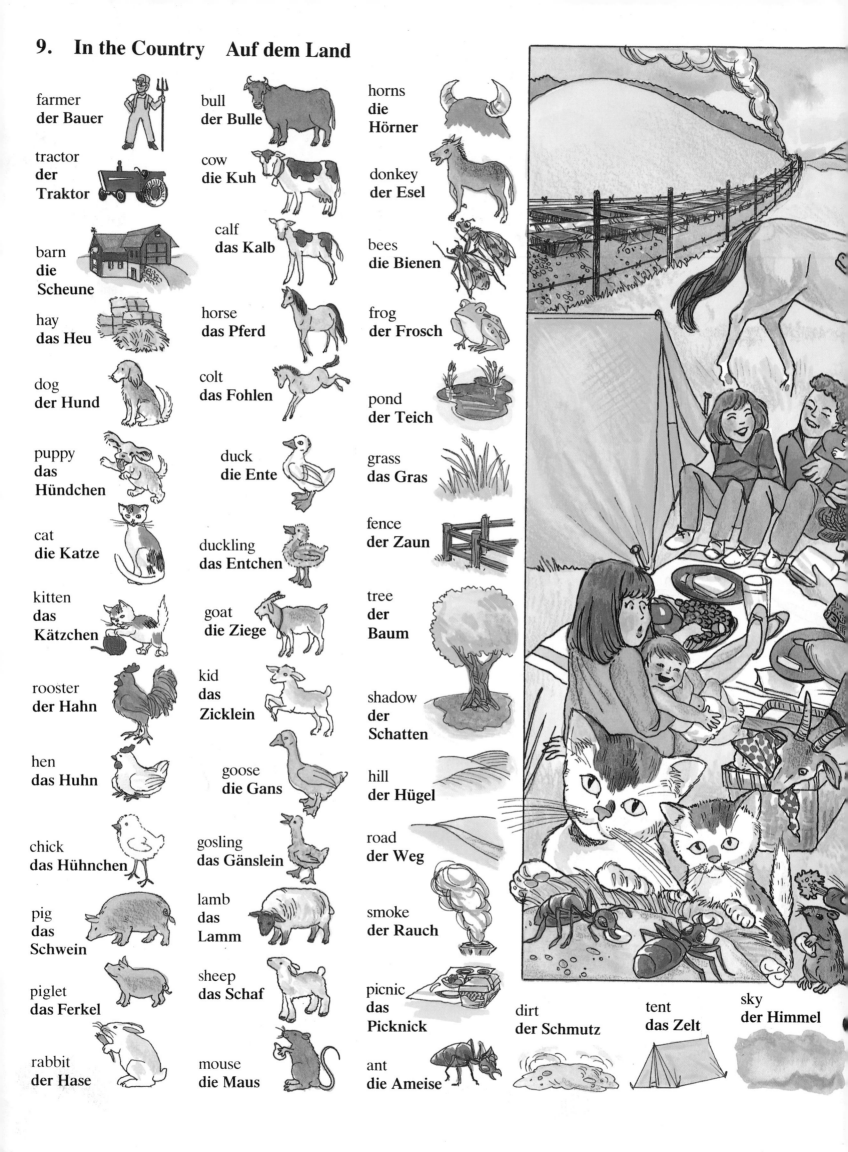

train tracks
die Gleise

sleeping bag
der Schlafsack

man
der Mann

woman
die Frau

boy
der Junge

girl
das Mädchen

baby
das Baby

farm
der Bauernhof

10. In a Restaurant   Im Restaurant

breakfast
das Frühstück

lunch
das Mittagessen

dinner
das Abendessen

yolk
das Eigelb

hamburger
der Hamburger

steak
das Steak

omelet
das Omelett

sandwich
das Butterbrot

fish
der Fisch

toast
der Toast

french fries
die Pommes frites

ham
der Schinken

jam
die Konfitüre

soup
die Suppe

chicken
das Hühnerfleisch

sausages
die Würste

noodles
die Nudeln

broccoli
die Brokkoli

coffee
der Kaffee

ketchup
der Ketchup

celery
der Sellerie

tea
der Tee

mustard
der Senf

salad
der Salat

cream
die Sahne

salt
das Salz

rice
der Reis

sugar
der Zucker

pepper
der Pfeffer

mushroom
der Pilz

meals
die Mahlzeiten

ice cream
das Eis

tray
das Tablett

waiter
der Kellner

candle
die Kerze

tablecloth
die Tischdecke

waitress
die Kellnerin

cake
der Kuchen

straw
der Trinkhalm

gift
das Geschenk

birthday party
die Geburtstagsfeier

soft drink
die Limonade

knife
das Messer

fork
die Gabel

spoon
der Löffel

plate
der Teller

saucer
die Untertasse

cup
die Tasse

glass
das Glas

bowl
die Schüssel

napkin
die Serviette

menu
die Speisekarte

11. The Doctor's Office   Beim Arzt

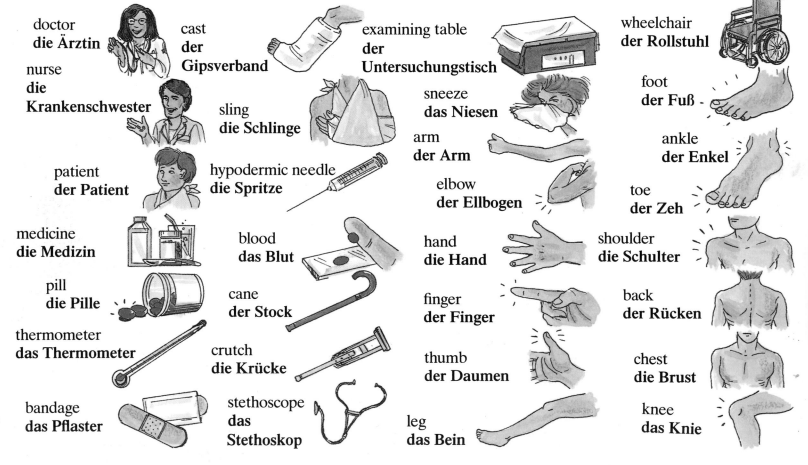

doctor
die Ärztin

nurse
die Krankenschwester

patient
der Patient

medicine
die Medizin

pill
die Pille

thermometer
das Thermometer

bandage
das Pflaster

cast
der Gipsverband

sling
die Schlinge

hypodermic needle
die Spritze

blood
das Blut

cane
der Stock

crutch
die Krücke

stethoscope
das Stethoskop

examining table
der Untersuchungstisch

sneeze
das Niesen

arm
der Arm

elbow
der Ellbogen

hand
die Hand

finger
der Finger

thumb
der Daumen

leg
das Bein

wheelchair
der Rollstuhl

foot
der Fuß

ankle
der Enkel

toe
der Zeh

shoulder
die Schulter

back
der Rücken

chest
die Brust

knee
das Knie

The Dentist's Office   Beim Zahnarzt

dentist
der Zahnarzt

waiting room
das Wartezimmer

eyebrow
die Augenbraue

braces
die Klammern

dental hygienist
die Zahnassistentin

magazines
die Zeitschriften

eyes
die Augen

head
der Kopf

tooth
der Zahn

X ray
die Röntgenstrahlen

nose
die Nase

face
das Gesicht

toothbrush
die Zahnbürste

smile
das Lächeln

mouth
der Mund

toothpaste
die Zahnpasta

lips
die Lippen

chin
das Kinn

cheek
die Wange

dental floss
der Zahnfaden

tongue
die Zunge

ear
das Ohr

forehead
die Stirn

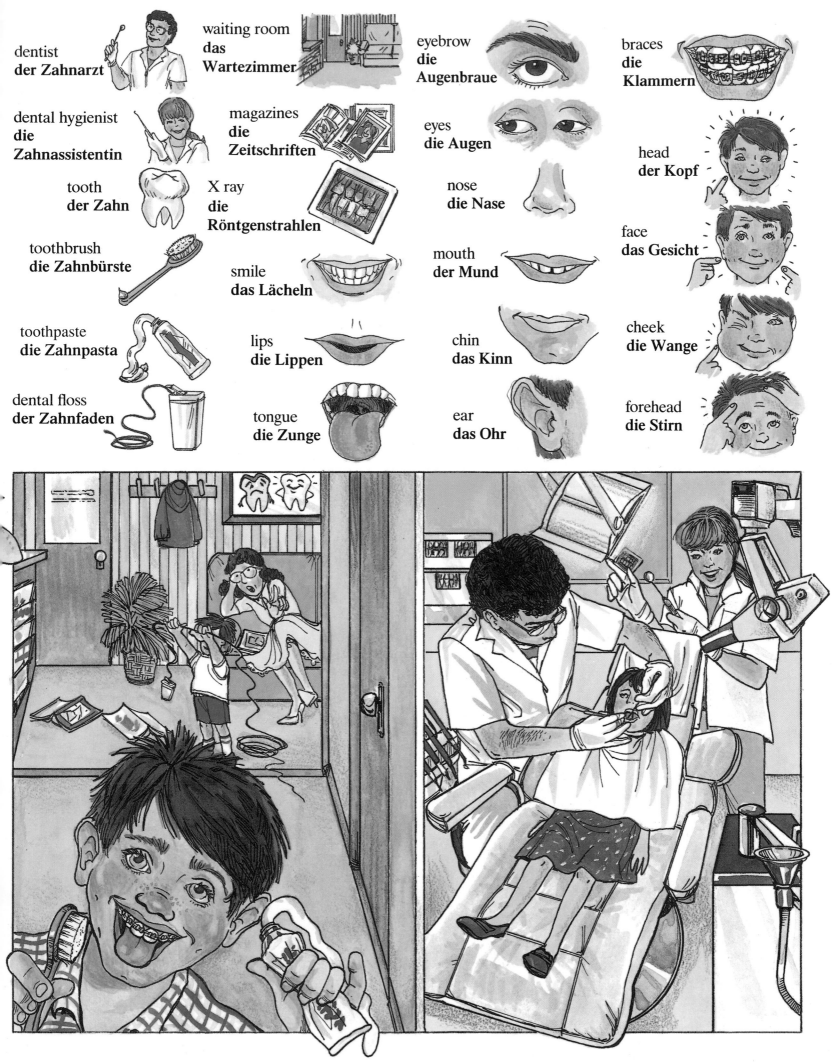

12. The Barber Shop/Beauty Salon
Beim Herrenfriseur/beim Damenfriseur

hairstylist
die Friseuse

mousse
der Schaum

barrette
die Haarspange

shampoo
das Shampoo

manicurist
die Handpflegerin

braid
der Zopf

suds
der Schaum

fingernail
der Fingernagel

wavy
wellig

comb
der Kamm

nail polish
der Nagellack

straight
glatt

brush
die Bürste

lipstick
der Lippenstift

curly
lockig

scissors
die Schere

mascara
das Maskara

short
kurz

curlers
die Lockenwickel

powder
der Puder

long
lang

curling iron
der Lockenstab

hair dryer
die Trockenhaube

black
schwarz

barber
der Herrenfriseur

bald
kahl

brown
braun

mustache
der Schnurrbart

shaving cream
die Rasiercreme

blond
blond

razor
das Rasiermesser

freckles
die Sommersprossen

red
rot

beard
der Bart

pedicurist
die Fußpflegerin

nail clippers
die Nagelschere

crew cut
der amerikanische Haarschnitt

nail file
die Nagelfeile

toenail
der Fußnagel

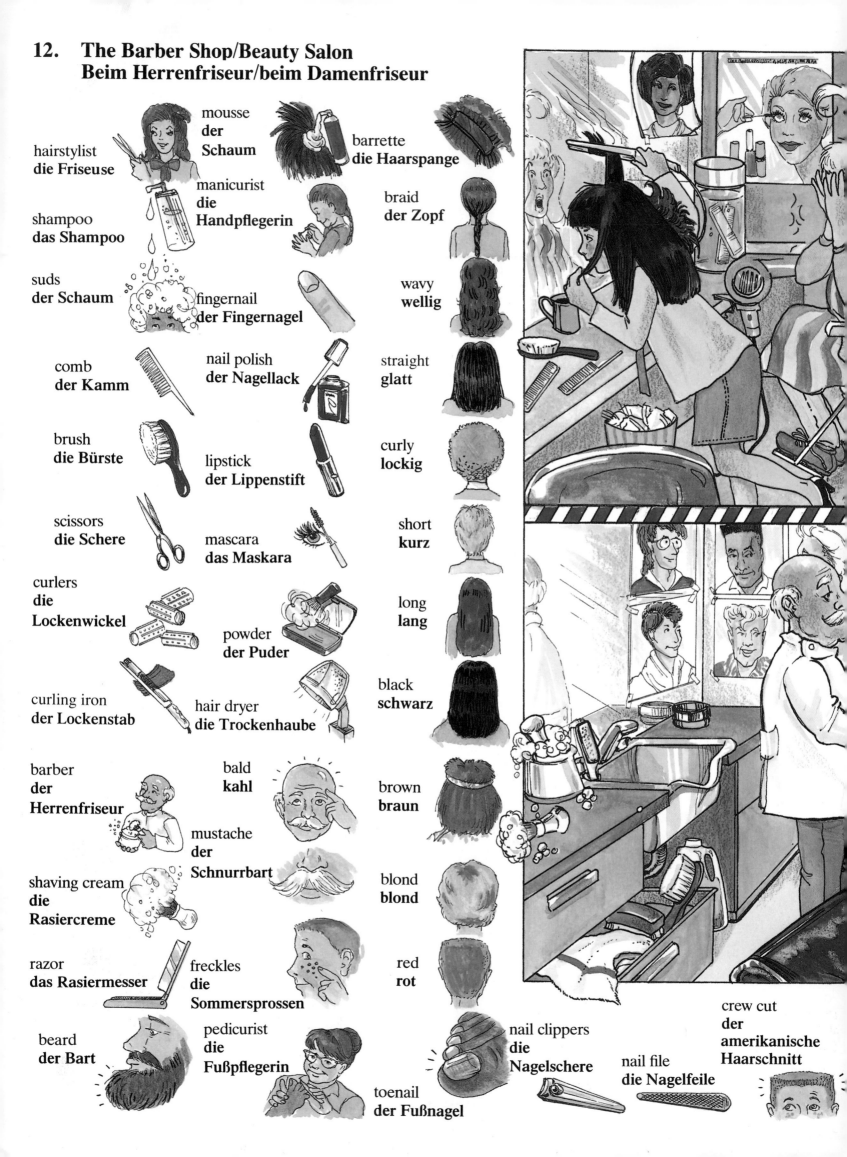

ponytail
der Pferdeschwanz

bangs
der Pony

bun
der Knoten

part
der Scheitel

hair spray
der Haarfestiger

hair
die Haare

blow dryer
der Fön

13. The Post Office   das Postamt

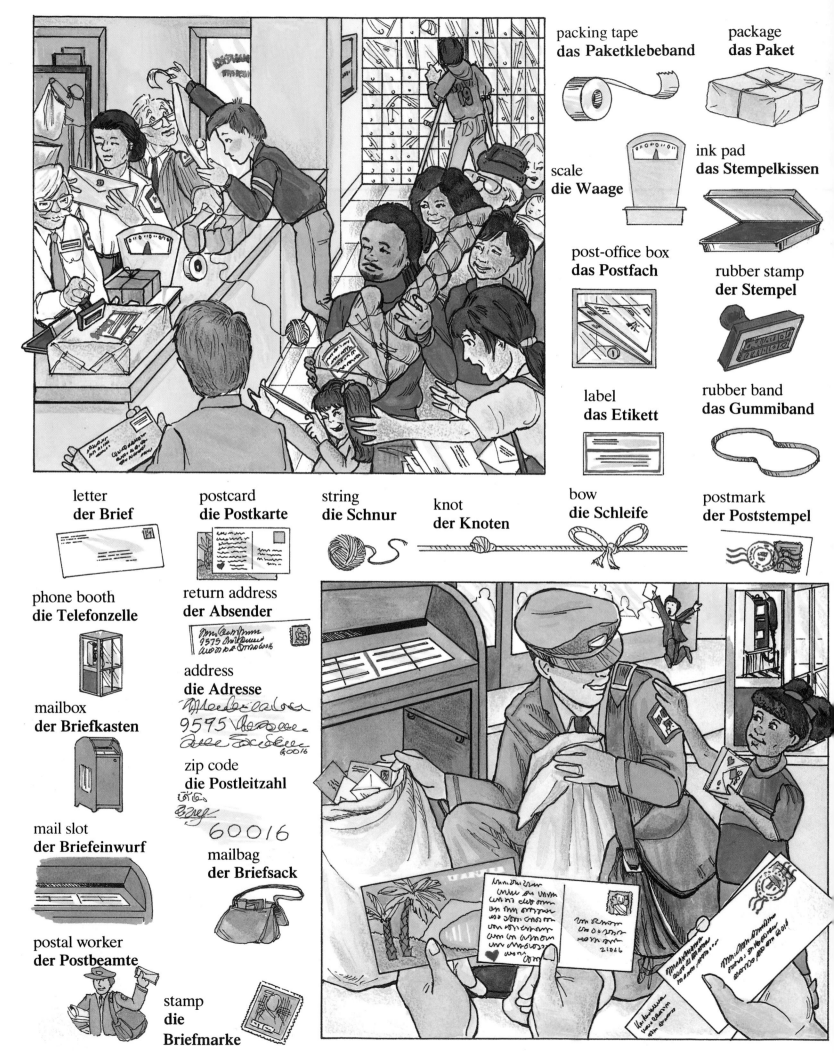

packing tape
das Paketklebeband

package
das Paket

scale
die Waage

ink pad
das Stempelkissen

post-office box
das Postfach

rubber stamp
der Stempel

label
das Etikett

rubber band
das Gummiband

letter
der Brief

postcard
die Postkarte

string
die Schnur

knot
der Knoten

bow
die Schleife

postmark
der Poststempel

phone booth
die Telefonzelle

return address
der Absender

address
die Adresse

zip code
die Postleitzahl

60016

mailbox
der Briefkasten

mail slot
der Briefeinwurf

mailbag
der Briefsack

postal worker
der Postbeamte

stamp
die Briefmarke

The Bank   die Bank

paper clip
die Büroklammer

security guard
die Wache

security camera
die Überwachungsanlage

safe
der Tresor

credit card
die Kreditkarte

typewriter
die Schreibmaschine

safety deposit box
das Bankschließfach

notepad
der Notizblock

teller
die Kassiererin

wallet
der Geldbeutel

key
der Schlüssel

lock
das Schloß

file cabinet
der Aktenschrank

receptionist
die Empfangsdame

bill
der Schein

coin
die Münze

check
der Scheck

checkbook
das Scheckbuch

piggy bank
das Sparschwein

signature
die Unterschrift

drive-in
der Autoschalter

automatic teller
der Geldautomat

14. At the Gas Station   Auf der Tankstelle

mechanic
der Mechaniker

coveralls
der Overall

gas pump
die Zapfsäule

race car
das Rennauto

pliers
die Zange

oil
das Öl

sunroof
das Schiebedach

dashboard
das Armaturenbrett

rag
der Lumpen

garage
die Garage

backseat
der Rücksitz

tow truck
der Abschlepper

car wash
die Autowaschanlage

driver's seat
der Fahrersitz

truck driver
der Lastwagenfahrer

gas cap
der Tankverschluß

passenger's seat
der Beifahrersitz

tank truck
der Tankwagen

tricycle
das Dreirad

seat belt
der Sitzgurt

bicycle
das Fahrrad

handlebars
die Lenkstange

hand brake
die Handbremse

reflectors
die Rückstrahler

hood
die Schutzhaube

bicycle chain
die Fahrradkette

pedal
das Pedal

engine
der Motor

kickstand
der Fahrradstand

trunk
der Kofferraum

spokes
die Speichen

fender
der Kotflügel

training wheels
die Stützräder

jack
der Wagenheber

flat tire
die Panne

tire
der Reifen

hubcap
die Nabe

headlight
der Scheinwerfer

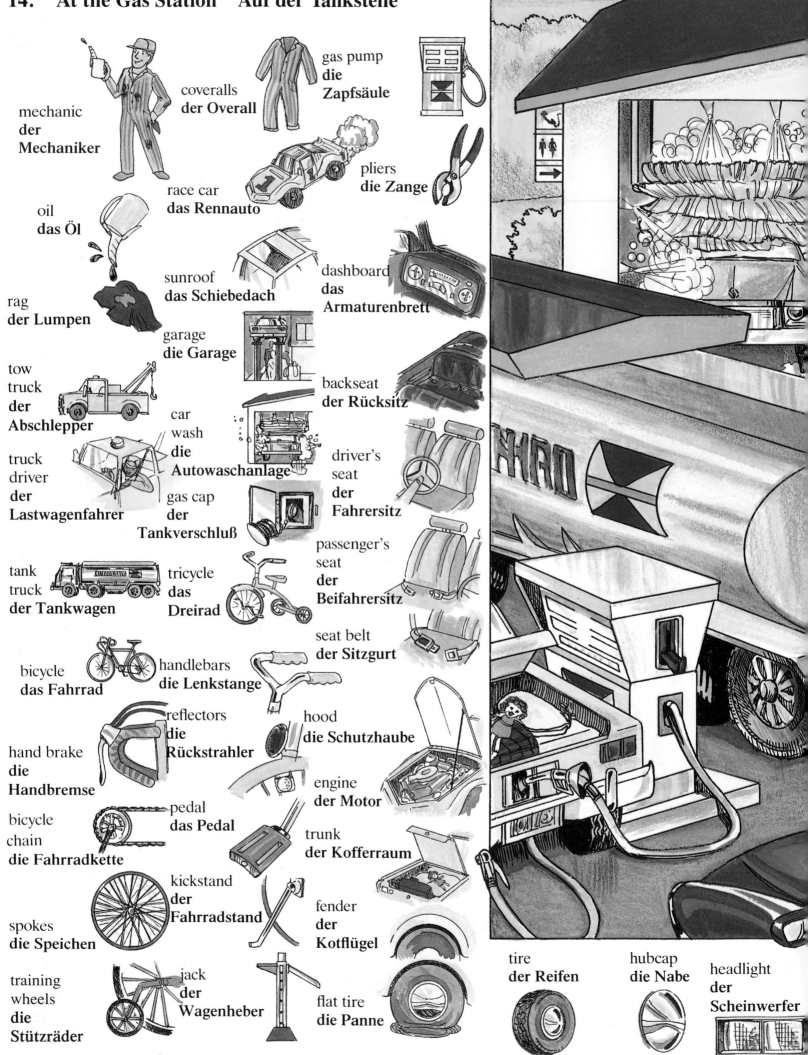

brake lights
die Bremslichter

windshield
die Windschutzscheibe

windshield wipers
die Scheibenwischer

steering wheel
das Lenkrad

rearview mirror
der Rückspiegel

air hose
der Luftschlauch
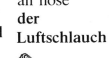

door handle
der Türgriff

15. People in Our Community   Leute in unserer Umgebung

saleswoman
die Verkäuferin

judge
die Richterin

cook
der Koch

model
das Mannequin

electrician
der Elektriker

fire fighter
der Feuerwehrmann

athlete
der Sportler

architect
die Architektin

doorman
der Portier

bus driver
die Busfahrerin

plumber
der Installateur

television repairer
der Fernsehmechaniker

taxi driver
der Taxifahrer

fashion designer
die Modeschöpferin

tour guide
die Fremdenführerin

bookseller
der Buchhändler

librarian
der Bibliothekar

computer programmer
die Komputerprogrammiererin

photographer
der Fotograf

gardener
der Gärtner

painter
der Anstreicher

salesman
der Verkäufer

secretary
die Sekretärin

weather forecaster
der Wetteransager

veterinarian
die Tierärztin

policewoman
die Polizistin

disc jockey
der Discjockey

reporter
der Reporter

construction worker
der Bauarbeiter

florist
die Blumenhändlerin

tailor
der Schneider

factory worker
die Fabrikarbeiterin

butcher
der Metzger

optician
die Optikerin

jeweler
der Juwelier

foreman
der Bauleiter

carpenter
der Schreiner

artist
die Künstlerin

pharmacist
die Apothekerin

sailor
der Matrose

banker
die Bankbeamtin

lawyer
die Rechtsanwältin

paramedic
der Arzthelfer

letter carrier
der Briefträger

fisherman
der Fischer

cowboy
der Cowboy

astronomer
der Astronom

policeman
der Polizist

16. Going Places (Transportation)
Unterwegs (Transport)

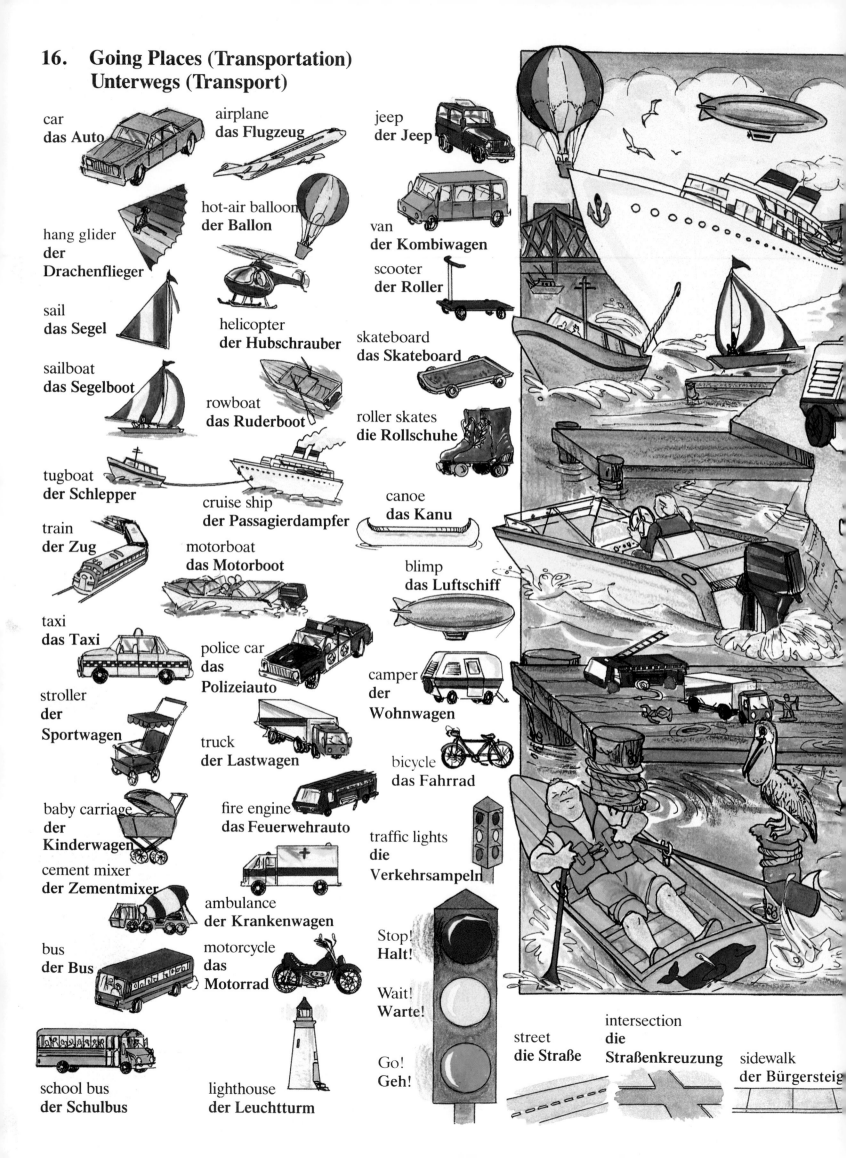

car
das Auto

airplane
das Flugzeug

jeep
der Jeep

hang glider
der Drachenflieger

hot-air balloon
der Ballon

van
der Kombiwagen

sail
das Segel

helicopter
der Hubschrauber

scooter
der Roller

sailboat
das Segelboot

rowboat
das Ruderboot

skateboard
das Skateboard

roller skates
die Rollschuhe

tugboat
der Schlepper

cruise ship
der Passagierdampfer

canoe
das Kanu

train
der Zug

motorboat
das Motorboot

blimp
das Luftschiff

taxi
das Taxi

police car
das Polizeiauto

camper
der Wohnwagen

stroller
der Sportwagen

truck
der Lastwagen

bicycle
das Fahrrad

baby carriage
der Kinderwagen

fire engine
das Feuerwehrauto

traffic lights
die Verkehrsampeln

cement mixer
der Zementmixer

ambulance
der Krankenwagen

Stop!
Halt!

bus
der Bus

motorcycle
das Motorrad

Wait!
Warte!

school bus
der Schulbus

lighthouse
der Leuchtturm

Go!
Geh!

street
die Straße

intersection
die Straßenkreuzung

sidewalk
der Bürgersteig

dock
der Pier

bus stop
die Bushaltestelle

bridge
die Brücke

crosswalk
der Fußgängerübergang

oar
das Ruder

boat
das Boot

stop sign
das Stopschild

17. The Airport der Flughafen

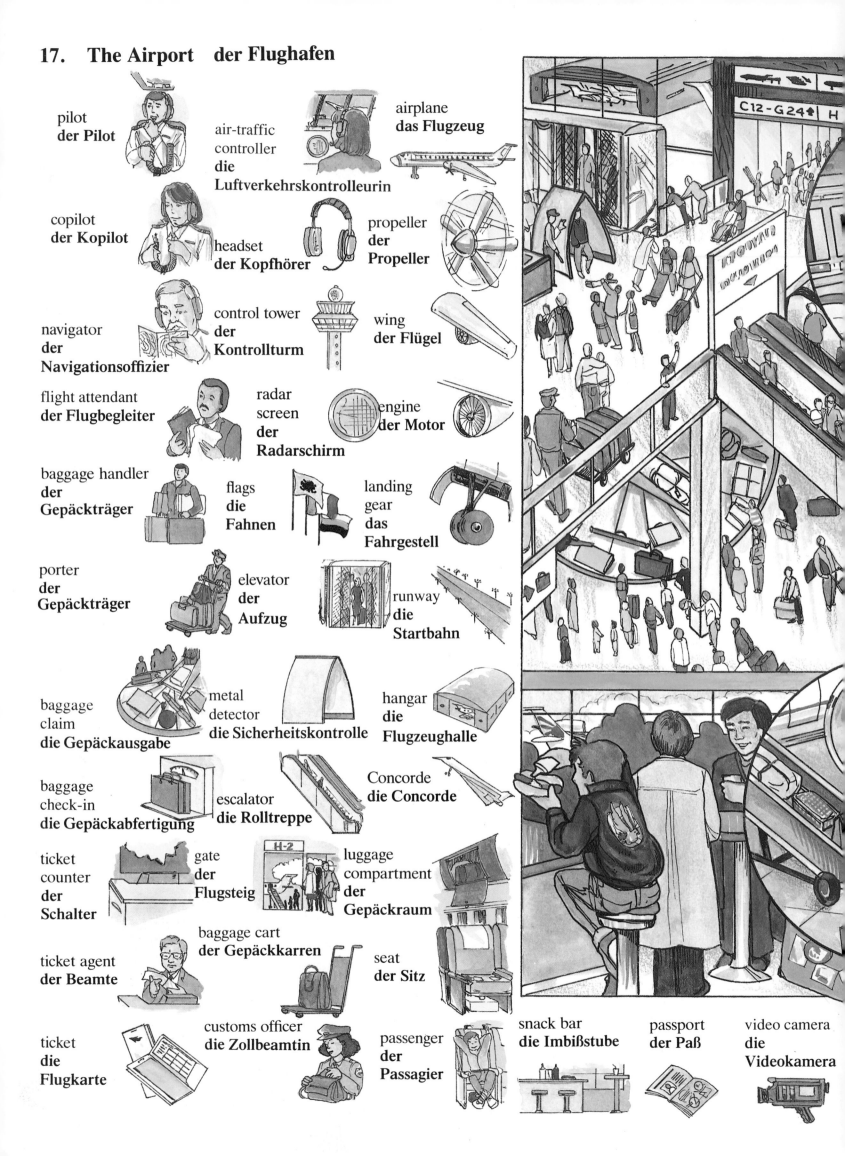

pilot **der Pilot**

air-traffic controller **die Luftverkehrskontrolleurin**

airplane **das Flugzeug**

copilot **der Kopilot**

headset **der Kopfhörer**

propeller **der Propeller**

navigator **der Navigationsoffizier**

control tower **der Kontrollturm**

wing **der Flügel**

flight attendant **der Flugbegleiter**

radar screen **der Radarschirm**

engine **der Motor**

baggage handler **der Gepäckträger**

flags **die Fahnen**

landing gear **das Fahrgestell**

porter **der Gepäckträger**

elevator **der Aufzug**

runway **die Startbahn**

baggage claim **die Gepäckausgabe**

metal detector **die Sicherheitskontrolle**

hangar **die Flugzeughalle**

baggage check-in **die Gepäckabfertigung**

escalator **die Rolltreppe**

Concorde **die Concorde**

ticket counter **der Schalter**

gate **der Flugsteig**

luggage compartment **der Gepäckraum**

ticket agent **der Beamte**

baggage cart **der Gepäckkarren**

seat **der Sitz**

ticket **die Flugkarte**

customs officer **die Zollbeamtin**

passenger **der Passagier**

snack bar **die Imbißstube**

passport **der Paß**

video camera **die Videokamera**

tennis racket
der Tennisschläger

binoculars
das Fernglas

camera
die Kamera

purse
die Handtasche

suitcase
der Koffer

garment bag
der Kleidersack

briefcase
die Aktentasche

18. Sports   der Sport

gymnastics
das Geräteturnen

goggles
die Schutzbrille

wrestling
das Ringen

cross-country skiing
der Langlauf

cycling
das Radfahren

soccer
das Fußballspiel

long jump
der Weitsprung

car racing
das Autorennen

baseball
der Baseball

boxing
das Boxen

badminton
das Federballspiel

net
das Netz

football
das amerikanische Fußballspiel

skates
die Schlittschuhe

skating
das Eislaufen

hurdles
das Hürdenrennen

golf
das Golfspiel

medal
die Medaille

horseback riding
das Reiten

baseball
das Baseballspiel

jogging
das Joggen

hockey
das Hockey

tennis
das Tennisspiel

diving
das Tauchen

weight lifting
das Gewichtheben

umpire
der Schiedsrichter

bowling
das Kegeln

boxing gloves
die Boxhandschuhe

high jump
der Hochsprung

table tennis
das Tischtennisspiel

skydiving
das Fallschirmspringen

soccer ball
der Fußball

at
er Baseballschläger

football
der amerikanische Fußball

parachute
der Fallschirm

swimming pool
das Schwimmbad

running
das Laufen

downhill skiing
der Abfahrtslauf

golf club
der Golfschläger

trophy
die Trophäe

horse racing
das Pferderennen

helmet
der Helm

bicycle
das Fahrrad

skis
die Schier

racket
der Schläger

sailing
das Segeln

basketball
das Korbballspiel

volleyball
das Volleyballspiel

referee
der Schiedsrichter

swimming
das Schwimmen

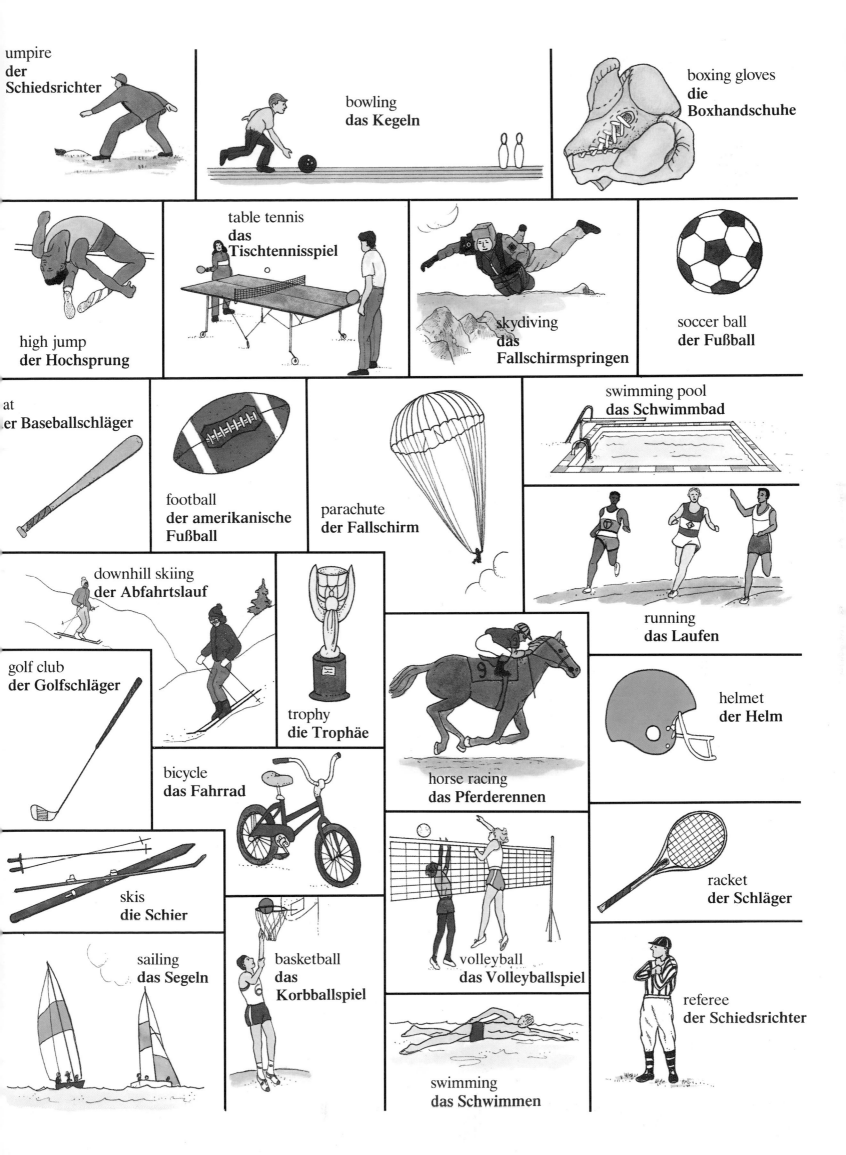

19. The Talent Show   der Wettbewerb

actor
der Schauspieler

actress
die Schauspielerin

children
die Kinder

auditorium
die Aula

audience
die Zuhörer

singer
der Sänger

stage
die Bühne

curtain
der Vorhang

dancer
die Tänzerin

scenery
die Kulisse

script
das Drehbuch

ballet slippers
die Ballettschuhe

spotlight
der Scheinwerfer

dressing room
das Ankleidezimmer

tutu
das Tanzkostüm

rope
das Seil

sewing machine
die Nähmaschine

leotard
das Trikot

microphone
das Mikrofon

master of ceremonies
der Programmleiter

costume
das Kostüm

makeup
die Schminke

orchestra pit
der Orchesterraum

mask
die Maske

sheet music
die Noten

orchestra
das Orchester

wig
die Perücke

conductor
der Dirigent

accordion
das Akkordeon

cymbals
die Becken

trumpet
die Trompete

saxophone
das Saxophon

French horn
das Waldhorn

piano
das Klavier

xylophone
das Xylophon

violin
die Geige

bow
der Bogen

guitar
die Guitarre

drum
die Trommel

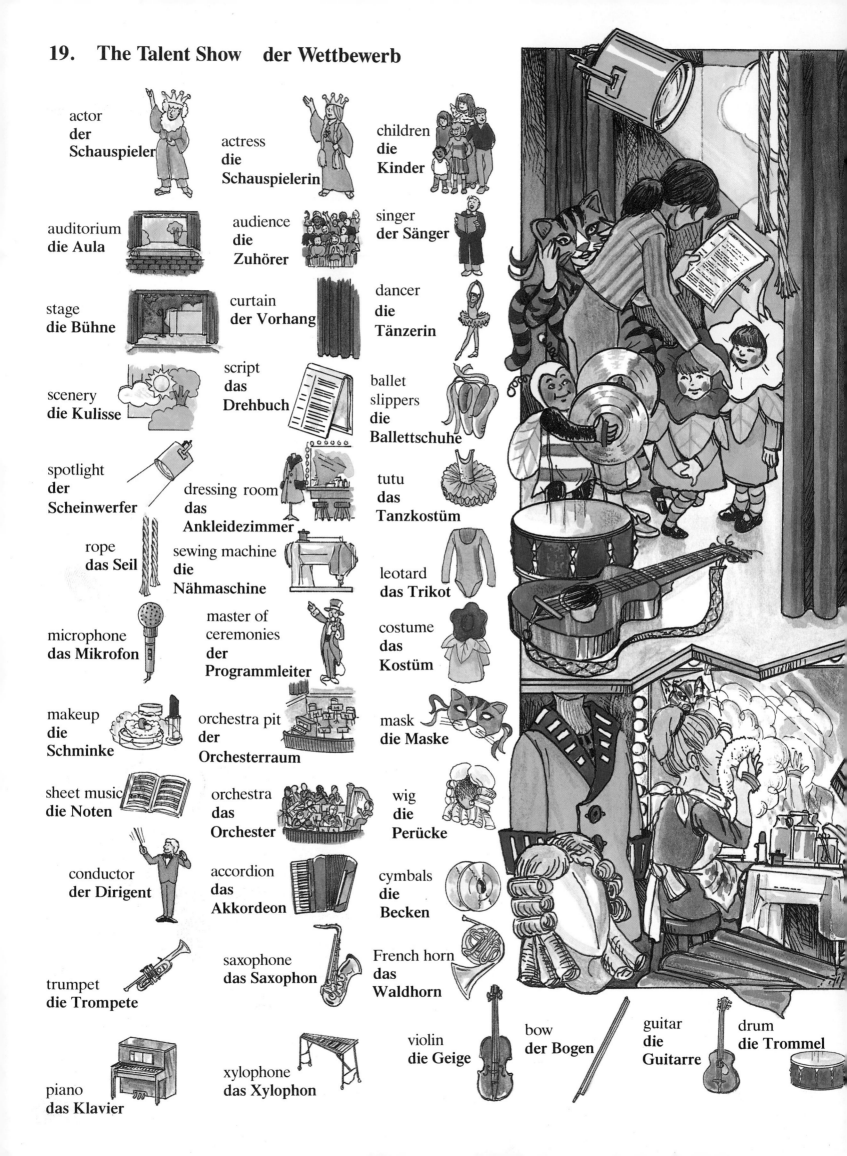

tuba
die Tuba

flute
die Flöte

trombone
die Posaune

clarinet
die Klarinette

cello
das Cello

strings
die Saiten

harp
die Harfe

20. At the Zoo Im Zoo

zookeeper
der Tierpfleger

elephant
der Elefant

animals
die Tiere

rhinoceros
das Nashorn

ostrich
der Strauß

fox
der Fuchs

lion
der Löwe

bear
der Bär

wolf
der Wolf

tiger
der Tiger

bear cub
das Bärchen

alligator
der Alligator

tiger cub
das Tigerjunge

polar bear
der Eisbär

zebra
das Zebra

jaguar
der Jaguar

panda
der Panda

giraffe
die Giraffe

leopard
der Leopard

gorilla
der Gorilla

monkey
der Affe

parrot
der Papagei

hippopotamus
das Flußpferd

flamingo
der Flamingo

owl
die Eule

snake
die Schlange

kangaroo
das Känguruh

swan
der Schwan

seal
die Robbe

deer
das Reh

penguin
der Pinguin

walrus
das Walroß

lizard
die Eidechse

peacock
der Pfau

hump
der Höcker

turtle
die Schildkröte

eagle
der Adler

camel
das Kamel

horns
die Hörner

wings
die Flügel

feathers
die Federn

beak
der Schnabel

paw
die Tatze

claws
die Krallen

mane
die Mähne

tail
der Schwanz

hoof
der Huf

stripes
die Streifen

spots
die Flecken

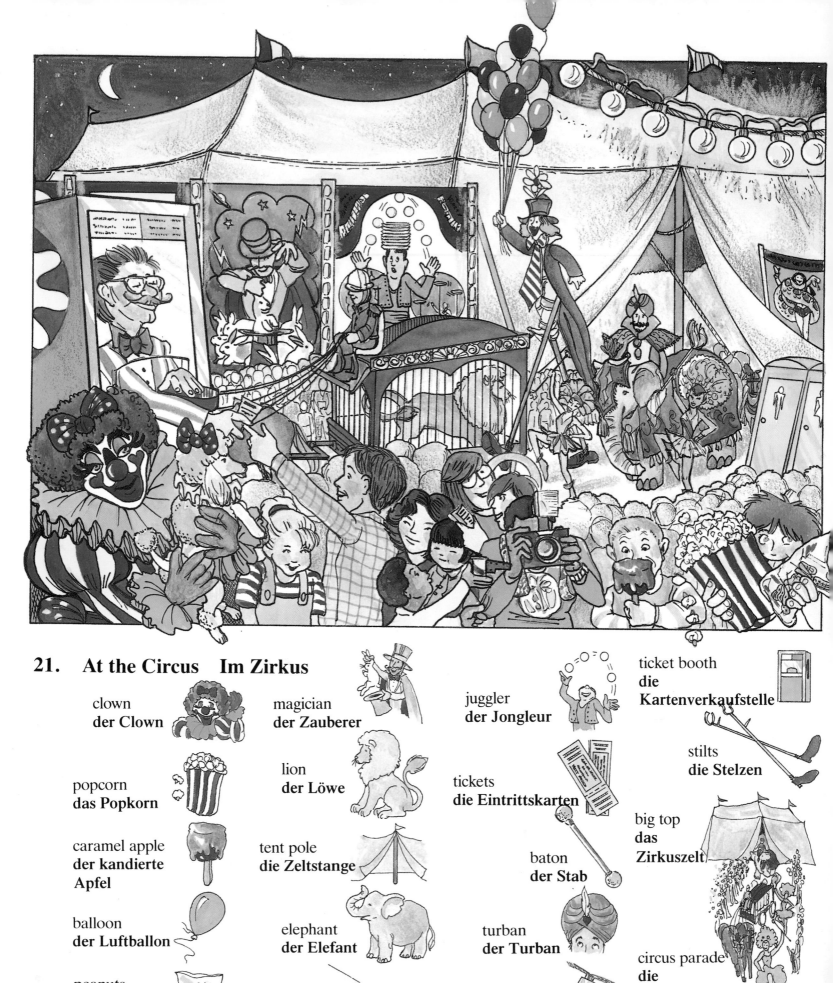

21. At the Circus   Im Zirkus

clown
der Clown

magician
der Zauberer

juggler
der Jongleur

ticket booth
die Kartenverkaufstelle

popcorn
das Popkorn

lion
der Löwe

tickets
die Eintrittskarten

stilts
die Stelzen

caramel apple
der kandierte Apfel

tent pole
die Zeltstange

baton
der Stab

big top
das Zirkuszelt

balloon
der Luftballon

elephant
der Elefant

turban
der Turban

peanuts
die Erdnüsse

flashbulb
das Blitzlicht

lightbulb
die Glühbirne

circus parade
die Zirkusparade

film
der Film

camera
die Kamera

night
die Nacht

rest rooms
die Toilette

bareback rider
die sattellose Reiterin

tightrope walker
die Drahtseilkünstlerin

trapeze
das Trapez

trapeze artist
der Trapezkünstler

tightrope
das Drahtseil

cage
der Käfig

band
das Orchester

safety net
das Sicherheitsnetz

whip
die Peitsche

lion tamer
der Löwenbändiger

unicycle
das Einrad

handstand
der Handstand

acrobat
der Artist

ring
die Manege

hoop
der Reifen

rope ladder
die Seilleiter

rope
das Seil

headstand
der Kopfstand

somersault
der Purzelbaum

cartwheel
das Rad

cotton candy
die Zuckerwatte

cape
das Cape

ringmaster
der Zirkusdirektor

22. In the Ocean
Im Ozean

scuba diver
der Taucher

wet suit
der Wasseranzug

flipper
die Schwimmflosse

oxygen tank
der Lufttank

snorkel
der Schnorchel

mask
die Tauchermaske

starfish
der Seestern

jellyfish
die Qualle

sea turtle
die Seeschildkröte

lobster
der Hummer

stingray
der Stechrochen

dolphin
der Delphin

shark
der Haifisch

octopus
der Seepolyp

tentacle
der Fangarm

swordfish
der Schwertfisch

angelfish
der Engelfisch

school (of fish)
der Zug

fishing line
die Angelschnur

fishhook
der Angelhaken

buoy
die Boje

submarine
das Unterseeboot

porthole
die Luke

sea urchin
der Seeigel

sea horse
das Seepferdchen

seaweed
der Seetang

shipwreck
der Schiffbruch

helm
der Helm

cannon
die Kanone

anchor
der Anker

treasure chest
die Schatzkiste

treasure
der Schatz

gold
das Gold

silver
das Silber

jewel
das Juwel

barnacle
die Entenmuschel

coral
die Koralle

coral reef
das Korallenriff

seashell
die Muschel

wave
die Welle

sand
der Sand

bubble
die Blase

scales
die Schuppen

gills
die Kiemen

fin
die Flosse

clam
die Muschel

crab
die Krabbe

squid
der Tintenfisch

whale
der Wal

23. Space
der Weltraum

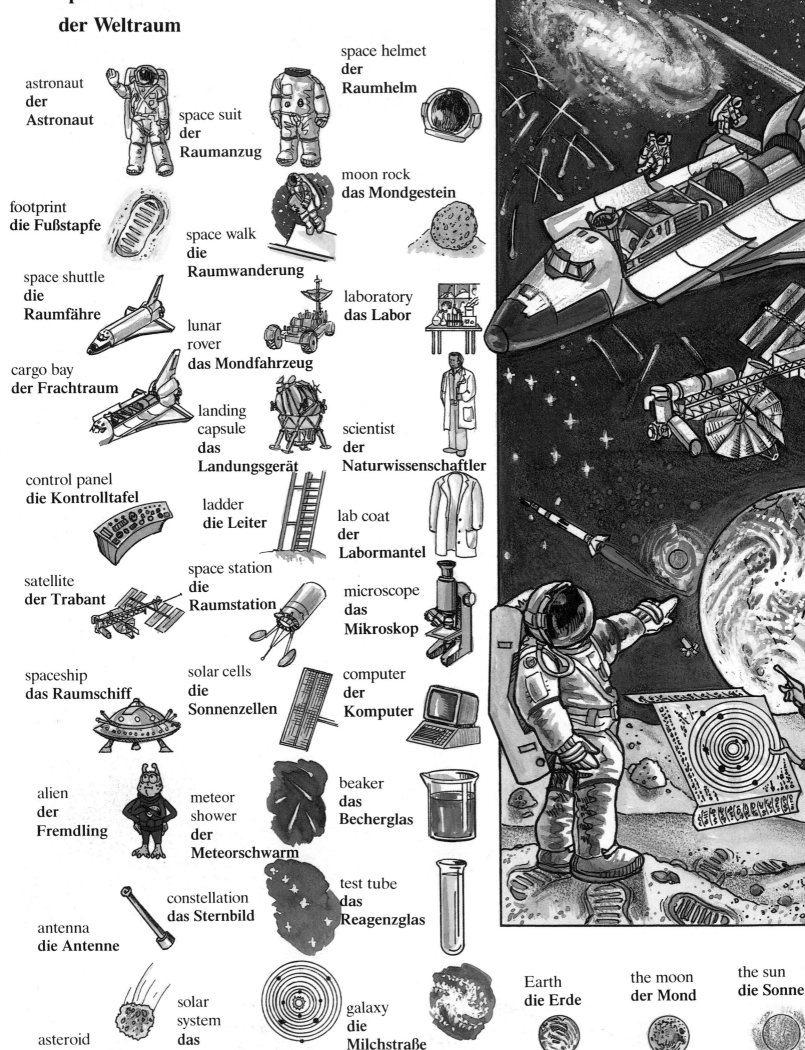

astronaut
der Astronaut

space suit
der Raumanzug

space helmet
der Raumhelm

footprint
die Fußstapfe

moon rock
das Mondgestein

space walk
die Raumwanderung

space shuttle
die Raumfähre

laboratory
das Labor

lunar rover
das Mondfahrzeug

cargo bay
der Frachtraum

landing capsule
das Landungsgerät

scientist
der Naturwissenschaftler

control panel
die Kontrolltafel

ladder
die Leiter

lab coat
der Labormantel

satellite
der Trabant

space station
die Raumstation

microscope
das Mikroskop

spaceship
das Raumschiff

solar cells
die Sonnenzellen

computer
der Komputer

alien
der Fremdling

meteor shower
der Meteorschwarm

beaker
das Becherglas

constellation
das Sternbild

test tube
das Reagenzglas

antenna
die Antenne

asteroid
der Asteroid

solar system
das Sonnensystem

galaxy
die Milchstraße

Earth
die Erde

the moon
der Mond

the sun
die Sonne

planet
der Planet

rings
die Höfe

crater
der Krater

stars
die Sterne

comet
der Komet

nebula
der Nebelfleck

rocket
die Rakete

robot
der Roboter

24. Human History
Menschheitsgeschichte

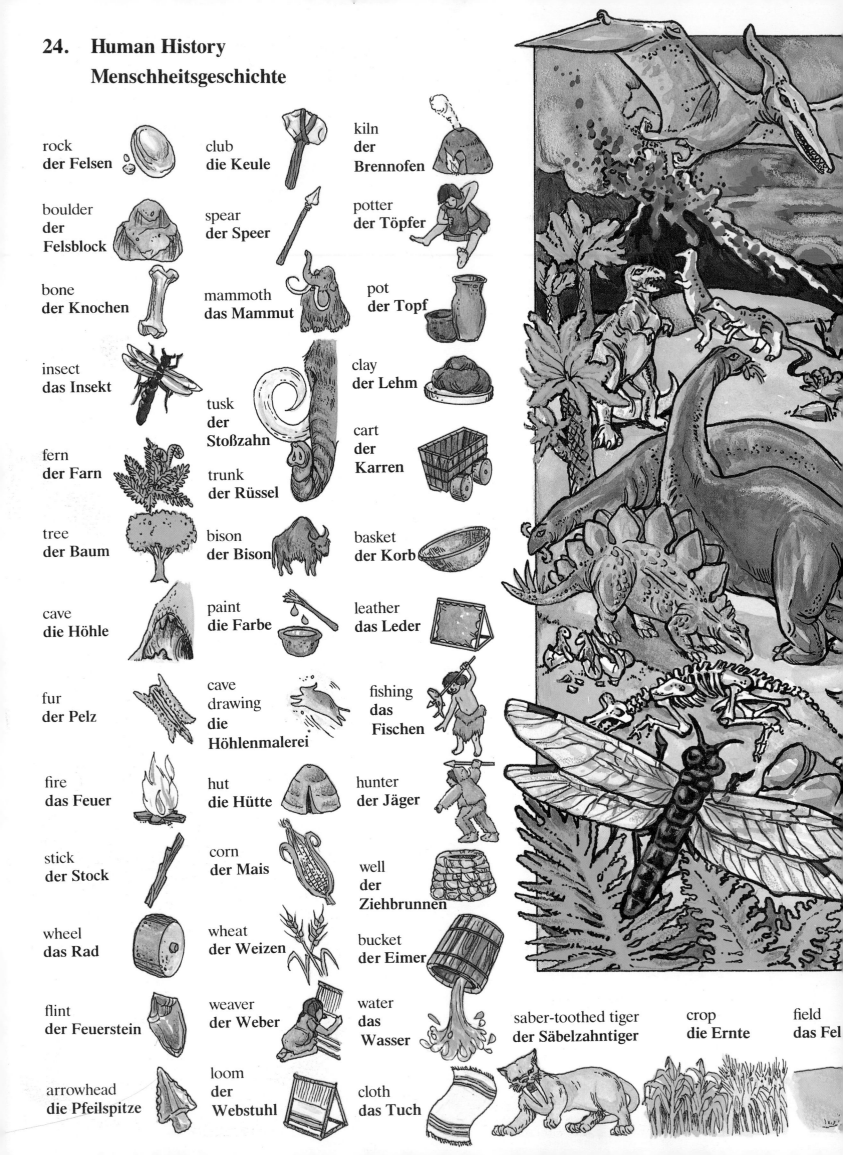

rock
der Felsen

boulder
der Felsblock

bone
der Knochen

insect
das Insekt

fern
der Farn

tree
der Baum

cave
die Höhle

fur
der Pelz

fire
das Feuer

stick
der Stock

wheel
das Rad

flint
der Feuerstein

arrowhead
die Pfeilspitze

club
die Keule

spear
der Speer

mammoth
das Mammut

tusk
der Stoßzahn

trunk
der Rüssel

bison
der Bison

paint
die Farbe

cave drawing
die Höhlenmalerei

hut
die Hütte

corn
der Mais

wheat
der Weizen

weaver
der Weber

loom
der Webstuhl

kiln
der Brennofen

potter
der Töpfer

pot
der Topf

clay
der Lehm

cart
der Karren

basket
der Korb

leather
das Leder

fishing
das Fischen

hunter
der Jäger

well
der Ziehbrunnen

bucket
der Eimer

water
das Wasser

cloth
das Tuch

saber-toothed tiger
der Säbelzahntiger

crop
die Ernte

field
das Fel

village
das Dorf

cave dwellers
die Höhlenbewohner

skeleton
das Skelett

dinosaur
der Dinosaurier

pterodactyl
der Flugsaurier

25. The Make-Believe Castle   das Märchenschloß

banner
das Banner

squire
der Edelknabe

court jester
der Hofnarr

dragon
der Drache

knight
der Ritter

minstrel
der Minnesänger

magic wand
der Zauberstab

armor
die Rüstung

unicorn
das Einhorn

fairy
die Fee

chain mail
das Kettenhemd

lance
die Lanze

elf
der Elf

forest
der Wald

shield
der Schild

giant
der Riese

saddle
der Sattel

ax
das Beil

forge
die Schmiede

stirrup
der Steigbügel

sword
das Schwert

blacksmith
der Hufschmied

reins
die Zügel

bow
der Bogen

anvil
der Amboß

stable
der Stall

arrow
der Pfeil

horseshoe
das Hufeisen

dungeon
der Kerker

quiver
der Köcher

tower
der Turm

moat
der Burggraben

archer
der Bogenschütze

courtyard
der Hof

drawbridge
die Zugbrücke

bat
die Fledermaus

rat
die Ratte

crown
die Krone

castle
das Schloß

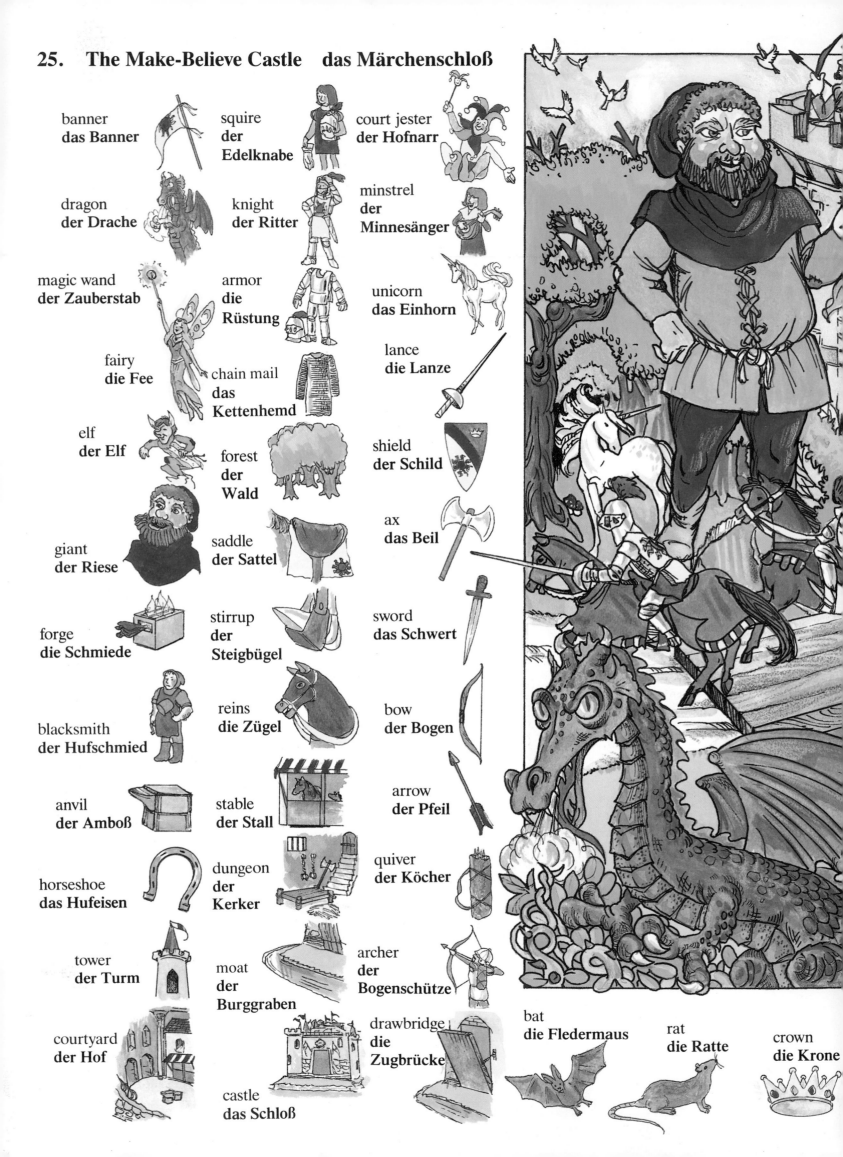

king
der König

queen
die Königin

princess
die Prinzessin

prince
der Prinz

throne
der Thron

spider
die Spinne

spiderweb
die Spinnwebe

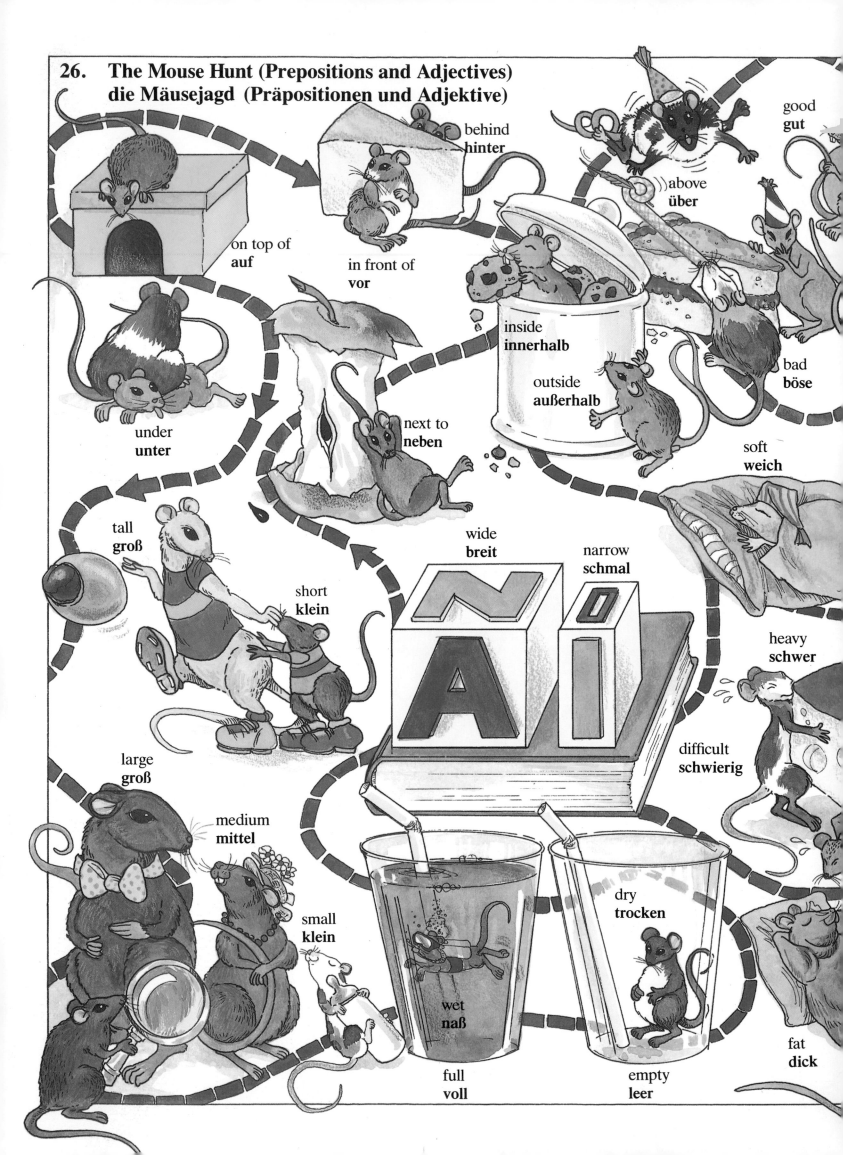

26. The Mouse Hunt (Prepositions and Adjectives)
die Mäusejagd (Präpositionen und Adjektive)

behind
hinter

good
gut

above
über

on top of
auf

in front of
vor

inside
innerhalb

outside
außerhalb

bad
böse

under
unter

next to
neben

soft
weich

tall
groß

wide
breit

narrow
schmal

short
klein

heavy
schwer

large
groß

difficult
schwierig

medium
mittel

dry
trocken

small
klein

wet
naß

full
voll

empty
leer

fat
dick

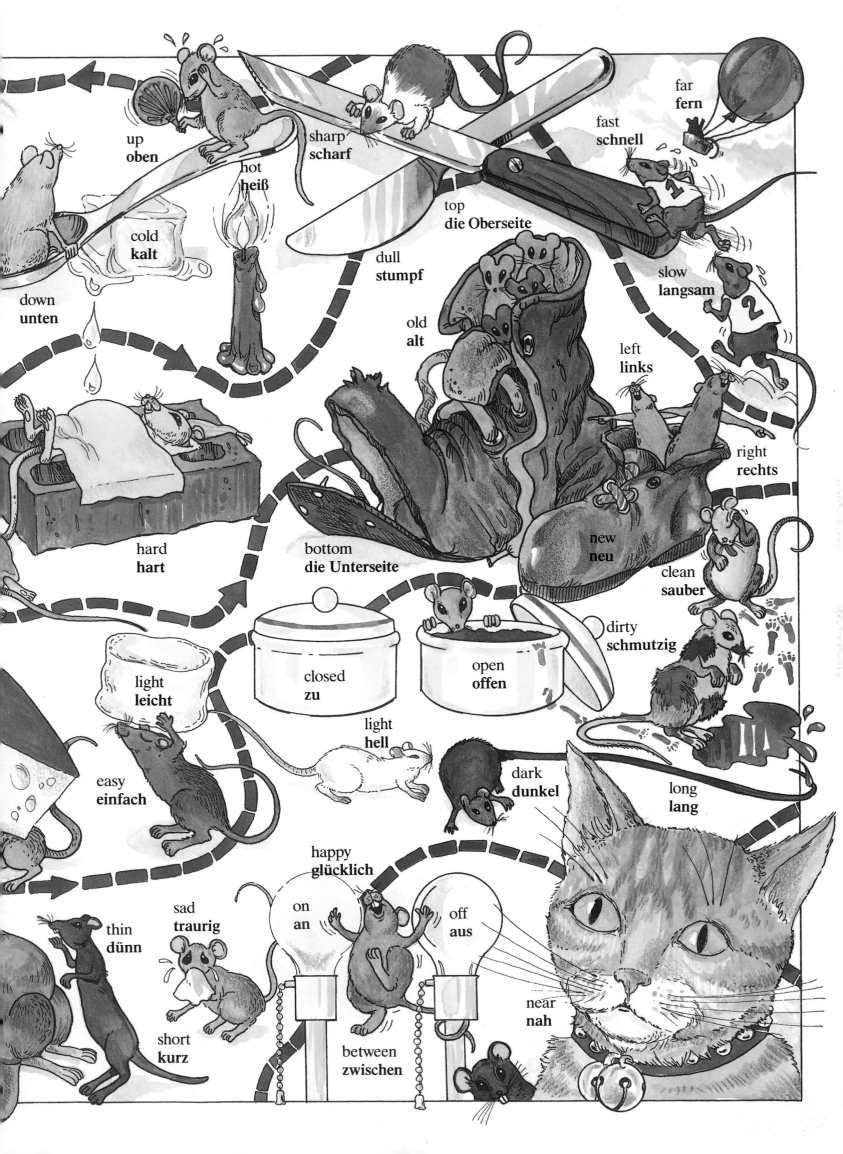

27. Action Words   Tätigkeitswörter

to drink **trinken**

to eat **essen**

to sleep **schlafen**

to wash **waschen**

to skate **eislaufen**

to fall **fallen**

to cry **weinen**

to laugh **lachen**

to fly **fliegen**

to write **schreiben**

to read **lesen**

to play (a game) **spielen**

to play (an instrument) **spielen**

to sit down **sich hinsetzen**

to stand up **aufstehen**

to dance **tanzen**

to walk **zu Fuß gehen**

to run **laufen**

to climb **klettern**

to jump **springen**

to drive **fahren**

to push **schieben**

to sell **verkaufen**

to buy **kaufen**

to ski **schifahren**

to dive **tauchen**

to swim **schwimmen**

to paint **malen**

to draw **zeichnen**

to ride a bicycle **Fahrrad fahren**

to come
kommen

to go
gehen

to throw
werfen

to catch
fangen

to watch
anschauen

to sing
singen

to talk
reden

to kick
~~kieken~~ stoßen

to listen (to)
zuhören

to think
denken

to roar
brüllen

to dig
graben

to pour
gießen

to juggle
jonglieren

to point (at)
deuten (auf)

to look for
suchen

to find
finden

to give
geben

to receive
bekommen

to cut
schneiden

to cook
kochen

to open
öffnen

to close
zumachen

to take a bath
baden

to teach
lehren

to break
brechen

to fix
reparieren

to carry
tragen

to pull
ziehen

to wait
warten

28. Colors die Farben

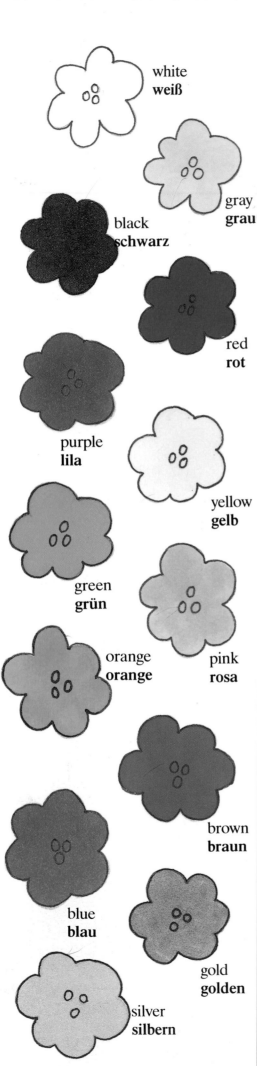

white
weiß

gray
grau

black
schwarz

red
rot

purple
lila

yellow
gelb

green
grün

orange
orange

pink
rosa

brown
braun

blue
blau

gold
golden

silver
silbern

29. The Family Tree der Stammbaum

grandmother, grandma
die Großmutter, Oma

father, dad
der Vater, Vati

mother, mom
die Mutter, Mutti

son
der Sohn

brother
der Bruder

sister
die Schwester

grandfather, grandpa
der Großvater, Opa

uncle
der Onkel

aunt
die Tante

cousin
der Cousin

cousin
die Kusine

daughter
die Tochter

square
das Viereck

triangle
das Dreieck

circle
der Kreis

rectangle **das Rechteck**

oval
das Oval

cube
der Würfel

octagon
das Achteck

sphere
die Kugel

cylinder
der Zylinder

cone
der Kegel

31. Numbers   die Nummern

Ordinal Numbers
die Ordnungszahlen

tenth
zehnt-

ninth
neunt-

eighth
acht-

sixth
sechst-

seventh
siebt-

fifth
fünft-

fourth
viert-

second
zweit-

third
dritt-

first
erst-

Cardinal Numbers
die Grundzahlen

0	½	1	2	3	4	5	6
zero	one-half	one	two	three	four	five	six
null	**ein halb**	**eins**	**zwei**	**drei**	**vier**	**fünf**	**sechs**

16	17	18	19	20	21
sixteen	seventeen	eighteen	nineteen	twenty	twenty-one
sechzehn	**siebzehn**	**achtzehn**	**neunzehn**	**zwanzig**	**einundzwanzig**

28	29	30	31
twenty-eight	twenty-nine	thirty	thirty-one
achtundzwanzig	**neunundzwanzig**	**dreißig**	**einunddreißig**

37	38	39	40
thirty-seven	thirty-eight	thirty-nine	forty
siebenunddreißig	**achtunddreißig**	**neununddreißig**	**vierzig**

46	47	48	49
forty-six	forty-seven	forty-eight	forty-nine
sechsundvierzig	**siebenundvierzig**	**achtundvierzig**	**neunundvierzig**

55	56	57	58
fifty-five	fifty-six	fifty-seven	fifty-eight
fünfundfünfzig	**sechsundfünfzig**	**siebenundfünfzig**	**achtundfünfzig**

64	65	66	67
sixty-four	sixty-five	sixty-six	sixty-seven
vierundsechzig	**fünfundsechzig**	**sechsundsechzig**	**siebenundsechzig**

73	74	75	76
seventy-three	seventy-four	seventy-five	seventy-six
dreiundsiebzig	**vierundsiebzig**	**fünfundsiebzig**	**sechsundsiebzig**

82	83	84	85
eighty-two	eighty-three	eighty-four	eighty-five
zweiundachtzig	**dreiundachtzig**	**vierundachtzig**	**fünfundachtzig**

91	92	93	94
ninety-one	ninety-two	ninety-three	ninety-four
einundneunzig	**zweiundneunzig**	**dreiundneunzig**	**vierundneunzig**

100	1,000	10,000
one hundred	one thousand	ten thousand
hundert	**tausend**	**zehntausend**

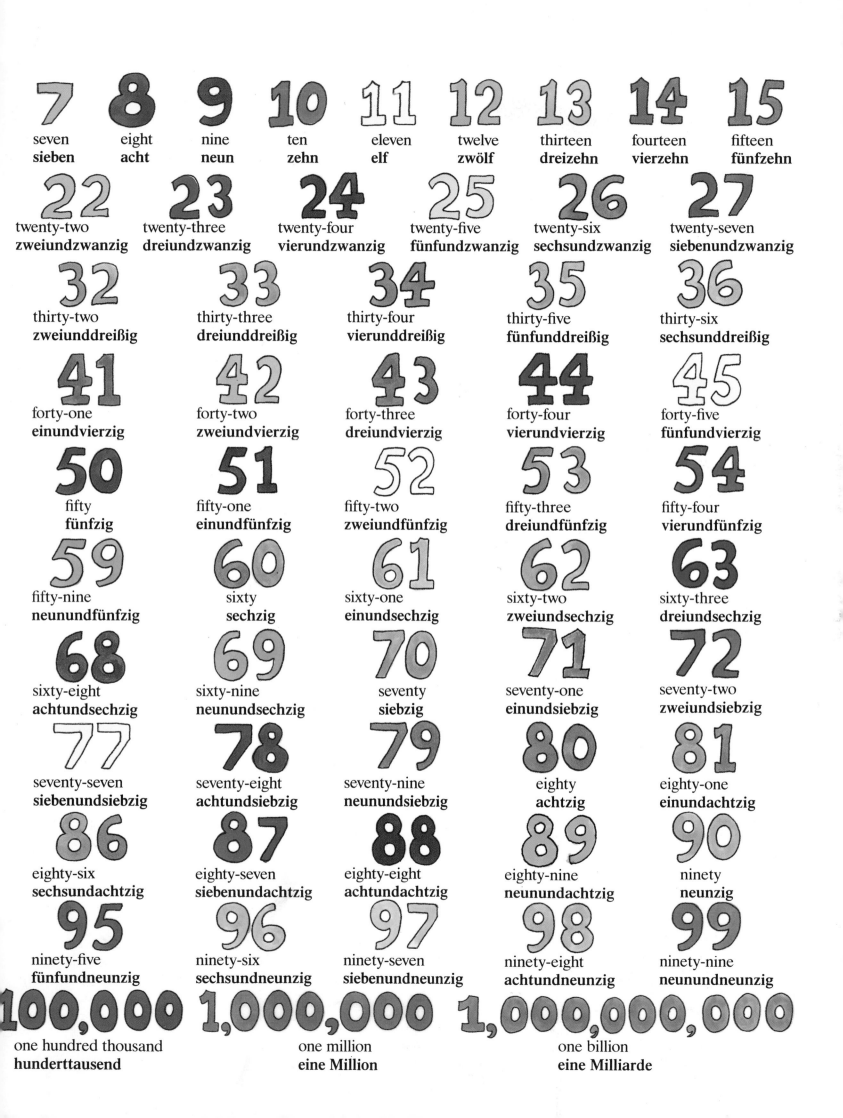

7	8	9	10	11	12	13	14	15
seven	eight	nine	ten	eleven	twelve	thirteen	fourteen	fifteen
sieben	**acht**	**neun**	**zehn**	**elf**	**zwölf**	**dreizehn**	**vierzehn**	**fünfzehn**

22	23	24	25	26	27
twenty-two	twenty-three	twenty-four	twenty-five	twenty-six	twenty-seven
zweiundzwanzig	**dreiundzwanzig**	**vierundzwanzig**	**fünfundzwanzig**	**sechsundzwanzig**	**siebenundzwanzig**

32	33	34	35	36
thirty-two	thirty-three	thirty-four	thirty-five	thirty-six
zweiunddreißig	**dreiunddreißig**	**vierunddreißig**	**fünfunddreißig**	**sechsunddreißig**

41	42	43	44	45
forty-one	forty-two	forty-three	forty-four	forty-five
einundvierzig	**zweiundvierzig**	**dreiundvierzig**	**vierundvierzig**	**fünfundvierzig**

50	51	52	53	54
fifty	fifty-one	fifty-two	fifty-three	fifty-four
fünfzig	**einundfünfzig**	**zweiundfünfzig**	**dreiundfünfzig**	**vierundfünfzig**

59	60	61	62	63
fifty-nine	sixty	sixty-one	sixty-two	sixty-three
neunundfünfzig	**sechzig**	**einundsechzig**	**zweiundsechzig**	**dreiundsechzig**

68	69	70	71	72
sixty-eight	sixty-nine	seventy	seventy-one	seventy-two
achtundsechzig	**neunundsechzig**	**siebzig**	**einundsiebzig**	**zweiundsiebzig**

77	78	79	80	81
seventy-seven	seventy-eight	seventy-nine	eighty	eighty-one
siebenundsiebzig	**achtundsiebzig**	**neunundsiebzig**	**achtzig**	**einundachtzig**

86	87	88	89	90
eighty-six	eighty-seven	eighty-eight	eighty-nine	ninety
sechsundachtzig	**siebenundachtzig**	**achtundachtzig**	**neunundachtzig**	**neunzig**

95	96	97	98	99
ninety-five	ninety-six	ninety-seven	ninety-eight	ninety-nine
fünfundneunzig	**sechsundneunzig**	**siebenundneunzig**	**achtundneunzig**	**neunundneunzig**

100,000	1,000,000	1,000,000,000
one hundred thousand	one million	one billion
hunderttausend	**eine Million**	**eine Milliarde**

32. A Map of the World   die Weltkarte

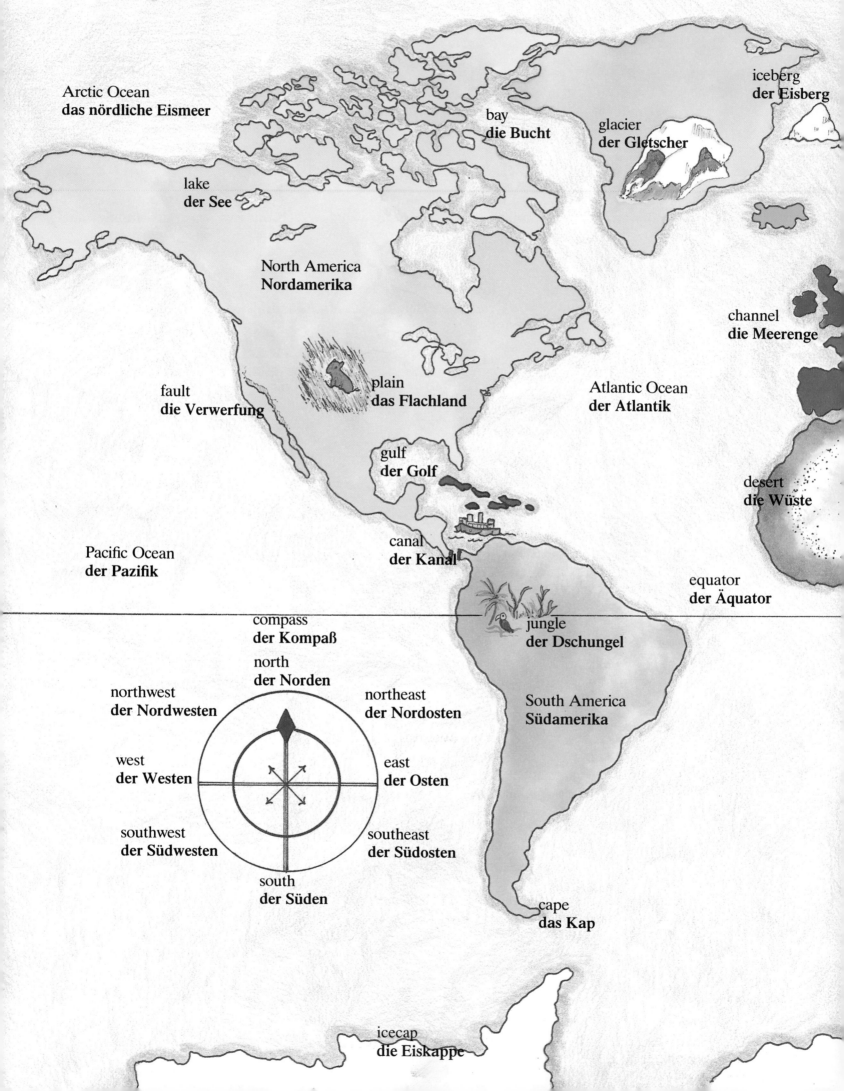

Arctic Ocean
das nördliche Eismeer

bay
die Bucht

glacier
der Gletscher

iceberg
der Eisberg

lake
der See

North America
Nordamerika

channel
die Meerenge

fault
die Verwerfung

plain
das Flachland

Atlantic Ocean
der Atlantik

desert
die Wüste

gulf
der Golf

canal
der Kanal

equator
der Äquator

Pacific Ocean
der Pazifik

jungle
der Dschungel

compass
der Kompaß

north
der Norden

northwest
der Nordwesten

northeast
der Nordosten

South America
Südamerika

west
der Westen

east
der Osten

southwest
der Südwesten

southeast
der Südosten

south
der Süden

cape
das Kap

icecap
die Eiskappe

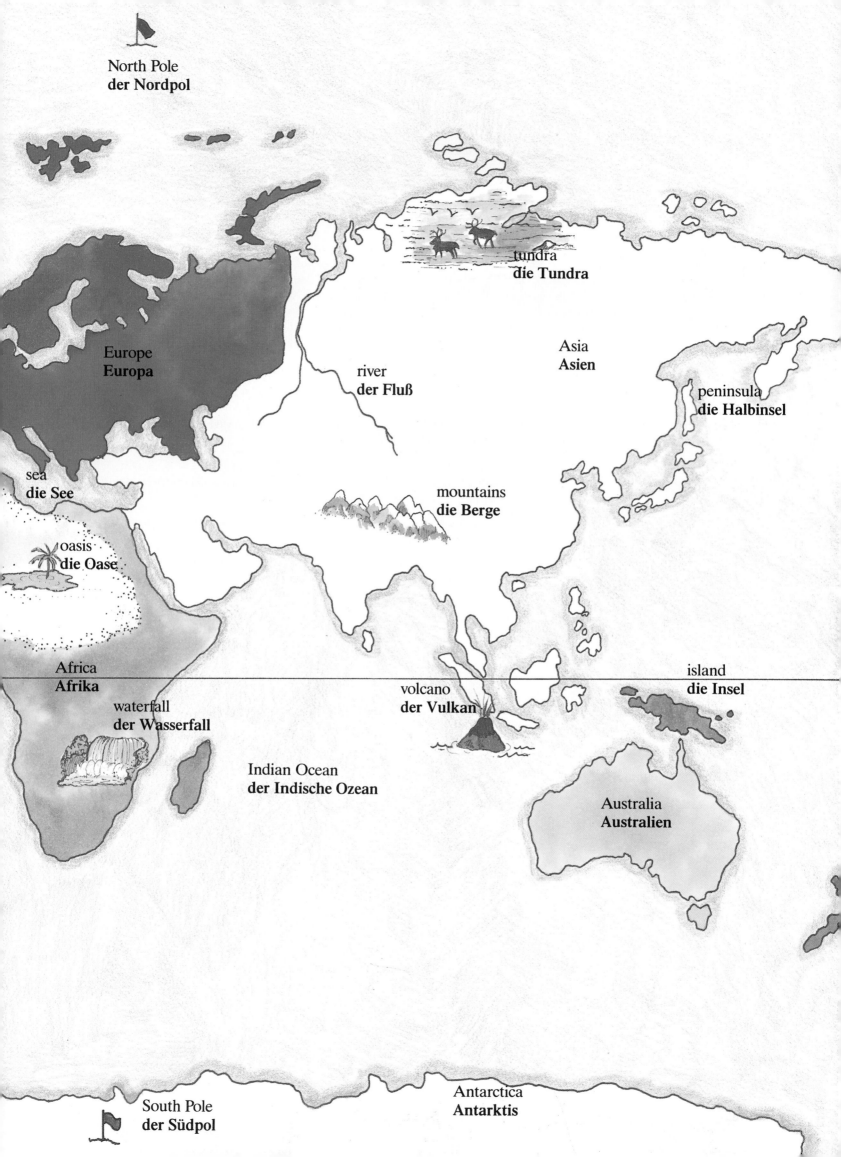

North Pole
der Nordpol

tundra
die Tundra

Asia
Asien

peninsula
die Halbinsel

Europe
Europa

river
der Fluß

sea
die See

mountains
die Berge

oasis
die Oase

Africa
Afrika

island
die Insel

waterfall
der Wasserfall

volcano
der Vulkan

Indian Ocean
der Indische Ozean

Australia
Australien

Antarctica
Antarktis

South Pole
der Südpol

German-English Glossary and Index

How to Say the Words in German

One of the most difficult things about learning a language is the pronunciation, how to say the words in the language. That's why we've written pronunciation guides to help you say the words in this book correctly. You will find a pronunciation guide after each German word in the *German-English Glossary and Index*. It may look funny, but if you read it aloud, you will be saying the word correctly.

German has some sounds that are not found in English. We have used capital letters for these sounds in the pronunciation guides to help you spot them easily. The German *r* (*R* in the pronunciation guides) has a sound that is not found in English. Say this sound at the back of your throat, a little like gargling. When you see *ER* in the pronunciation guides, say the sound by shaping your lips as if to make the *oh* sound and holding your tongue as if to make the *ay* sound. When you see *U* in the pronunciation guides, say the sound by shaping your lips as if to make the *oo* sound and holding your tongue as if to make the *ee* sound. To make the *H* sound, shape your mouth to make the *ee* sound and blow through it. It should sound a

little like *sh*, but much lighter. To make the *K* sound, say *k*, as in *duke*, but don't let your tongue touch the roof of your mouth; blow through it.

Here are a few more hints for using the pronunciation guides. Always pronounce *ow* like the *ow* in *now*. Always pronounce *igh* like the *i* in *night*. *Ah* always sounds like the *a* in *father* and *oh* always sounds like the *o* in *go*.

You may also notice that each word in the pronunciation guides has one syllable in heavy dark letters. This is the stressed syllable. When you say a word in English, you always say one syllable a little louder than the others. This is called the stressed syllable. When you read the pronunciation guides aloud, just say the syllables in heavy dark letters a little louder than the others to use the correct stress.

After the pronunciation guide, the *German-English Glossary and Index* gives the English meaning for each word and the number of the picture where you can find the word.

einundsechzig (ighn-oont-**zeK**-tsiH), sixty-one, 31

einundsiebzig (ighn-oont-**zeep**-tsiH), seventy-one, 31

einundvierzig (ighn-oont-**feeR**-tsiH), forty-one, 31

einundzwanzig (ighn-oont-**tsvahn**-tsiH), twenty-one, 31

das Eis (dahs ighs), ice, 5; ice cream, 10

der Eisbär (daiR **ighs**-bayR), polar bear, 20

der Eisberg (daiR **ighs**-baiRg), iceberg, 32

die Eiskappe (dee **ighs**-kahp-puh), icecap, 32

eislaufen (**ighs**-low-fen), skate, 27

das Eislaufen (dahs **ighs**-low-fen), skating, 18

die Eiswürfel (dee **ighs**-vUR-fel), ice cubes, 3

der Eiszapfen (daiR **ighs**-tsahp-fen), icicle, 5

der Elefant (daiR **e**-le-fahnt), elephant, 20, 21

der Elektriker (daiR **e**-lek-tRi-keR), electrician, 15

der elektrische Zug (daiR **e**-lek-tRi-shuh tsook), electric train, 4

elf (elf), eleven, 31

der Elf (daiR elf), elf, 25

der Ellbogen (daiR **el**-boh-gen), elbow, 11

die Empfangsdame (dee emp-**fahngs**-dah-muh), receptionist, 13

der Engelfisch (daiR **en**-gel-fish), angelfish, 22

der Enkel (daiR **en**-kel), ankle, 11

das Entchen (dahs **ent**-Hen), duckling, 9

die Ente (dee **en**-tuh), duck, 9

die Entenmusche (dee **en**-ten-moo-shuh), barnacle, 22

die Erbsen (dee **aiRb**-sen), peas, 6

die Erdbeeren (dee **aiRd**-bai-Ren), strawberries, 6

die Erde (dee **aiR**-duh), Earth, 23

die Erdnüsse (dee **aiRd**-nUs-suh), peanuts, 21

die Ernte (dee **aiRn**-tuh), crop, 24

erst- (airst), first, 31

der Esel (daiR **ay**-zel), donkey, 9

essen (**es**-sen), eat, 27

das Essen (dahs **es**-sen), food, 6

das Eßzimmer (dahs **es**-tsim-meR), dining room, 2

das Etikett (dahs **e**-ti-ket), label, 13

die Eule (dee **oy**-luh), owl, 20

Europa (oy-**Roh**-pah), Europe, 32

die Fabrik (dee fah-**bReek**), factory, 8

die Fabrikarbeiterin (dee fah-**bReek**-ahR-bigh-te-Rin), factory worker, 15

der Fächer (daiR **fay**-HeR), fan, 4

die Fahnen (dee **fahn**-nen), flags, 17

fahren (**fah**-Ren), drive, 27

der Fahrersitz (daiR **fahR**-eR-zits), driver's seat, 14

das Fahrgestell (dahs **fahR**-ge-shtell), landing gear, 17

das Fahrrad (dahs **fahR**-Raht), bicycle, 14, 16, 18

Fahrrad fahren (**fahr**-Raht **fah**-Ren), ride a bicycle, 27

die Fahrradkette (dee **fahR**-Raht-ket-tuh), bicycle chain, 14

der Fahrradstand (daiR **fahR**-Raht-shtahnt), kickstand, 14

fallen (**fahl**-len), fall, 27

der Fallschirm (daiR **fahl**-sheeRm), parachute, 18

das Fallschirmspringen (dahs **fahl**-sheeRm-shpRin-gen), skydiving, 18

der Fangarm (daiR **fahng**-ahRm), tentacle, 22

fangen (**fahn**-gen), catch, 27

die Farbe (dee **fahR**-buh), paint, 1, 24

die Farben (dee **fahR**-ben), colors, 28

die Farbstifte (dee **fahRb**-shtif-tuh), colored pencils, 1

der Farn (daiR fahRn), fern, 24

die Fäustlinge (dee **foyst**-lin-guh), mittens, 7

die Feder (dee **fay**-deR), feather, 4

das Federballspiel (dahs **fay**-deR-bahl-shpeel), badminton, 18

die Federn (dee **fay**-deRn), feathers, 20

die Fee (dee fay), fairy, 25

der Feile (daiR **figh**-luh), file, 3

das Feld (dahs felt), field, 24

der Felsblock (daiR **felz**-blohk), boulder, 24

der Felsen (daiR **fel**-zen), rock, 24

das Fenster (dahs **fen**-steR), window, 2

das Ferkel (dahs **faiR**-kel), piglet, 9

fern (faiRn), far, 26

das Fernglas (dahs **faiRn**-glahs), binoculars, 17

der Fernseher (daiR **faiRn**-zay-er), television, 2

der Fernsehmechaniker (daiR **faiRn**-zay-me-kah-ni-keR), television repairer, 15

das Feuer (dahs **foy**-eR), fire, 24

der Feuerstein (daiR **foy**-eR-shtighn), flint, 24

das Feuerwehrauto (dahs **foy**-eR-vaiR-ow-toh), fire engine, 16

der Feuerwehrmann (daiR **foy**-eR-vaiR-mahn), fire fighter, 15

die Feuerwehrzentrale (dee **foy**-eR-vaiR-tsen-tRah-luh), fire station, 8

der Film (daiR film), film, 21

der Filmprojektor (daiR **film**-pRoh-yek-tohR), movie projector, 4

finden (**fin**-den), find, 27

der Finger (daiR **fin**-geR), finger, 11

der Fingernagel (daiR **fin**-geR-nah-gel), fingernail, 12

der Fisch (daiR fish), fish, 1, 10

das Fischen (dahs **fi**-shen), fishing, 24

der Fischer (daiR **fi**-sheR), fisherman, 15

das Flachland (dahs **flahK**-lahnt), plain, 32

der Flamingo (daiR **flah**-min-goh), flamingo, 20

die Flasche (dee **flah**-shuh), bottle, 6

die Flecken (dee **flek**-ken), spots, 20

die Fledermaus (dee **flay**-deR-mows), bat, 25

das Fleisch (dahs flighsh), meat, 6

die Fliege (dee **flee**-guh), fly, 5

fliegen (**flee**-gen), fly, 27

die Fliegenklatsche (dee **flee**-gen-klaht-shuh), fly swatter, 5

die Flosse (dee **flohs**-suh), fin, 22

die Flöte (dee **flER**-tuh), flute, 19

der Flugbegleiter (daiR **flook**-be-gligh-teR), flight attendant, 17

der Flügel (daiR **flU**-gel), wing, 17, 20

die Flügel (dee **flU**-gel), wings, 20

der Flughafen (daiR **flook**-hah-fen), airport, 17

die Flugkarte (dee **flook**-kahR-tuh), plane ticket, 17

der Flugsaurier (daiR **flook**-zow-Ree-eR), pterodactyl, 24

der Flugsteig (daiR **flook**-shtighk), gate, 17

das Flugzeug (dahs **flook**-tsoyk), airplane, 16, 17

die Flugzeughalle (dee **flook**-tsoyk-hahl-luh), hangar, 17

der Fluß (daiR floos), river, 32

das Flußpferd (dahs **floos**-pfaiRd), hippopotamus, 20

das Fohlen (dahs **foh**-len), colt, 9

der Fön (daiR fERn), blow dryer, 12

die Formen (dee **foR**-men), shapes, 30

das Fotoalbum (dahs **foh**-toh-ahl-boom), photo album, 4

der Fotograf (daiR foh-toh-**gRahf**), photographer, 15

der Frachtraum (daiR **fRahKt**-Rowm), cargo bay, 23

die Frau (dee fRow), woman, 9

die Fremdenführerin (dee **fRem**-den-fU-Re-Rin), tour guide, 15

der Fremdling (daiR **fRemt**-ling), alien, 23

die Friseuse (dee fRee-zERz), hairstylist, 12

die Frisierkommode (dee fRi-**zeeR**-kohm-moh-duh), dresser, 2

der Frosch (daiR **fRohsh**), frog, 9

der Fruchtsaft (daiR **fRooKt**-zahft), fruit juice, 6

der Frühling (daiR **frU**-ling), spring, 5

das Frühstück (dahs **fRU**-shtUk), breakfast, 10

der Fuchs (daiR **fooKs**), fox, 20

fünf (fUnf), five, 31

fünft- (fUnft), fifth, 31

fünfundachtzig (fUnf-oont-**ahKt**-tsiH), eighty-five, 31

fünfunddreißig (fUnf-oont-**dRigh**-tsiH), thirty-five, 31

fünfundfünfzig (fUnf-oont-**fUnf**-tsiH), fifty-five, 31

fünfundneunzig (fUnf-oont-**noyn**-tsiH), ninety-five, 31

fünfundsechzig (fUnf-oont-**zeK**-tsiH), sixty-five, 31

fünfundsiebzig (fUnf-oont-**zeep**-tsiH), seventy-five, 31

fünfundvierzig (fUnf-oont-**feeR**-tsiH), forty-five, 31

fünfundzwanzig (fUnf-oont-**tsvahn**-tsiH), twenty-five, 31

fünfzehn (**fUnf**-tsayn), fifteen, 31

fünfzig (**fUnf**-tsiH), fifty, 31

der Fuß (daiR foos), foot, 11

zu Fuß gehen (tsoo foos **gay**-en), walk, 27

der Fußball (daiR **foos**-bahl), soccer ball, 18

das Fußballspiel (dahs **foos**-bahl-shpeel), soccer, 18

der Fußbank (daiR **foos**-bahnk), footstool, 2

der Fußboden (daiR **foos**-boh-den), floor, 2

der Fußgängerübergang (daiR **foos**-gayn-geR-U-beR-gahng), crosswalk, 16

der Fußnagel (daiR **foos**-nah-gel), toenail, 12

die Fußpflegerin (dee **foos**-pflay-ge-Rin), pedicurist, 12

die Fußstapfe (dee **foos**-shtahp-fuh), footprint, 23

die Gabel (dee **gah**-bel), fork, 10

die Gans (dee gahns), goose, 9

das Gänslein (dahs **gayns**-lighn), gosling, 9

die Garage (dee gah-**Rah**-juh), garage, 14

das Garn (dahs gahRn), yarn, 4

der Gartenschlauch (daiR **gahR**-ten-shlowK), garden hose, 5

der Gärtner (daiR **gayRt**-neR), gardener, 15

das Gebäude (dahs ge-**boy**-duh), building, 8

geben (**gay**-ben), give, 27

die Geburtstagsfeier (dee ge-**booRts**-tahgs-figh-eR), birthday party, 10

das Gefängnis (dahs ge-**fayng**-nis), jail, 8

geh! (gay), Go!, 16

gehen (**gay**-en), go, 27

die Geige (dee **gigh**-guh), violin, 19

gelb (gelb), yellow, 28

das Geld (dahs gelt), money, 6

der Geldautomat (daiR **gelt**-ow-toh-maht), automatic teller, 13

der Geldbeutel (daiR **gelt**-boy-tel), wallet, 13

das Gemüse (dahs ge-**mU**-zuh), vegetables, 6

der Gemüsegarten (daiR ge-**mU**-ze-gahR-ten), vegetable garden, 5

die Gepäckabfertigung (dee ge-**payk**-ahp-**faiR**-ti-goong), baggage check-in, 17

die Gepäckausgabe (dee ge-**payk**-ows-gah-buh), baggage claim, 17

der Gepäckkarren (daiR ge-**payk**-kahR-Ren), baggage cart, 17

der Gepäckraum (daiR ge-**payk**-Rowm), luggage compartment, 17

der Gepäckträger (daiR ge-**payk**-tRay-geR), baggage handler, porter, 17

das Geräteturnen (dahs ge-**Ray**-te-tooR-nen), gymnastics, 18

das Geschenk (dahs ge-**shenk**), gift, 10

das Geschirr (dahs ge-**sheeR**), dishes, 3

das Gesicht (dahs ge-**ziHt**), face, 11

das Gewichtheben (dahs ge-**viHt**-hay-ben), weight lifting, 18

gießen (**gee**-sen), pour, 27

der Gipsverband (daiR **gips**-faiR-bahnd), cast, 11

die Giraffe (dee gee-**Rahf**-fuh), giraffe, 20

das Glas (dahs glahs), glass, 10

glatt (glaht), straight, 12

die Gleise (dee **gligh**-zuh), train tracks, 9

der Gletscher (daiR **glet**-sheR), glacier, 32

der Globus (daiR **gloh**-boos), globe, 1

die Glocke (dee **gloh**-kuh), bell, 1

glücklich (**glUk**-liH), happy, 26

die Glühbirne (dee **glU**-beeR-nuh), lightbulb, 4, 21

das Gold (dahs gohlt), gold, 22

golden (**gohl**-den), gold, 28

der Golf (daiR gohlf), gulf, 32

der Golfschläger (daiR **gohlf**-shlay-geR), golf club, 18

das Golfspiel (dahs **gohlf**-shpeel) golf, 18

der Gorilla (daiR goh-**Ril**-lah), gorilla, 20

graben (**gRah**-ben), dig, 27

das Gras (dahs grahs), grass, 9

grau (gRow), gray, 28

der Grill (daiR gRill), barbecue, 5

groß (gRohs), large, 26; tall, 26

die Großmutter (dee **gRohs**-moot-teR), grandmother, 29

der Großvater (daiR **gRohs**-fah-teR), grandfather, 29

grün (gRUn), green, 28

die Grundzahlen (dee **gRoont**-tsah-len), cardinal numbers, 31

die grünen Bohnen (dee **gRU**-nen **boh**-nen), green beans, 6

die Guitarre (dee gi-**tahR**-Ruh), guitar, 19

das Gummiband (dahs **goom**-mi-bahnt), rubber band, 13

der Gürtel (daiR **gUR**-tel), belt, 7

gut (goot), good, 26

die Haare (dee **hah**-Ruh), hair, 12

der Haarfestiger (daiR **hahR**-fe-sti-geR), hair spray, 12

die Haarspange (dee **hahR**-shpahn-guh), barrette, 12

der Hahn (daiR hahn), rooster, 9

der Haifisch (daiR **high**-fish), shark, 22

ein halb (ighn hahlb), one-half, 31

die Halbinsel (dee **hahlb**-in-zel), peninsula, 32

die Halskette (dee **hahls**-ket-tuh), necklace, 7

das Halstuch (dahs **hals**-tooK), scarf, 7

Halt! (hahlt), Stop!, 16

der Hamburger (daiR **hahm**-booR-geR), hamburger, 10

der Hammer (daiR **hahm**-meR), hammer, 3

die Hand (dee hahnt), hand, 11

die Handbremse (dee **hahnt**-bRem-zuh), hand brake, 14

die Handpflegerin (dee **hahnt**-pflay-ge-Rin), manicurist, 12

die Handpuppe (dee **hahnt**-poop-puh), puppet, 4

die Handschuhe (dee **hahnt**-shoo-huh), gloves, 7

der Handstand (daiR **hahnt**-shtahnt), handstand, 21

die Handtasche (dee **hahnt**-tah-shuh), purse, 17

das Handtuch (dahs **hahnt**-tooK), towel, 2

die Hängematte (dee **hayn**-ge-maht-tuh), hammock, 5

die Harfe (dee **hahR**-fuh), harp, 19

hart (hahRt), hard, 26

der Hase (daiR **hah**-zuh), rabbit, 9

das Haus (dahs hows), house, 2

die Hausapotheke (dee **hows**-ah-poh-tay-kuh), medicine cabinet, 2

das Heft (dahs heft), notebook, 1

die Heftklammern (dee **heft**-klahm-meRn), staples, 1

die Heftmaschine (dee **heft**-mah-shee-nuh), stapler, 1

heiß (highs), hot, 26

hell (hel), light, 26

der Helm (daiR helm), helm, 22; helmet, 18

das Hemd (dahs hemt), shirt, 7

der Herbst (daiR haiRbst), fall, 5

der Herd (daiR haiRt), stove, 3

der Herrenfriseur (daiR **haiR**-Ren-fRee-zUR), barber, 12

beim Herrenfriseur (bighm **haiR**-Ren-fRee-zUR), at the barber shop, 12

das Heu (dahs hoy), hay, 9

die Heuschrecke (dee **hoy**-shRek-kuh), grasshopper, 5

die Himbeeren (dee **him**-bay-Ren), raspberries, 6

der Himmel (daiR **him**-mel), sky, 9

hinter (**hin**-teR), behind, 26

der Hochsprung (daiR **hohK**-shpRoong), high jump, 18

der Höcker (daiR **hERk**-keR), hump, 20

das Hockey (dahs **hohk**-key), hockey, 18

der Hof (daiR hohf), courtyard, 25; yard, 5

die Höfe (dee **hER**-fuh), rings, 23

der Hofnarr (daiR **hohf**-nahR), court jester, 25

die Höhle (dee **hER**-luh), cave, 24

die Höhlenbewohner (dee **hER**-len-be-voh-neR), cave dwellers, 24

die Höhlenmalerei (dee **hER**-len-mah-le-Righ), cave drawing, 24

das Holz (dahs hohlts), wood, 3

der Holzlotz (daiR **hohlts**-lohts), log, 5

die Hörner (dee **hERR**-neR), horns, 9, 20

die Hosen (dee **hoh**-zen) pants, 7

das Hotel (dahs hoh-**tel**), hotel, 8

der Hubschrauber (daiR **hoop**-shRow-beR), helicopter, 16

der Huf (daiR hoof), hoof, 20

das Hufeisen (dahs **hoof**-igh-zen), horseshoe, 25

der Hufschmied (daiR **hoof**-shmeed), blacksmith, 25

der Hügel (daiR **hU**-gel), hill, 9

das Huhn (dahs hoon), hen, 9

das Hühnchen (dahs **hUn**-Hen), chick, 9

das Hühnerfleisch (dahs **hU**-neR-flighsh), chicken, 10

der Hummer (daiR **hoom**-meR), lobster, 22

der Hund (daiR hoont), dog, 9

das Hündchen (dahs **hUnt**-Hen), puppy, 9

hundert (**hoon**-daiRt), one hundred, 31

hunderttausend (hoon-daiRt-**tow**-zent), one hundred thousand, 31

das Hürdenrennen (dahs **hUR**-den-Ren-nen), hurdles, 18

der Hut (daiR hoot), hat, 4, 7

die Hütte (dee **hUt**-tuh), hut, 24

der Hydrant (daiR **hoo**-dRahnt), fire hydrant, 8

die Imbißstube (dee im-bis-shtoo-buh), snack bar, 17

der Indische Ozean (daiR in-di-shuh oh-tsee-ahn), Indian Ocean, 32

innerhalb (in-neR-hahlp), inside, 26

das Insekt (dahs in-zekt), insect, 24

die Insel (dee in-zel), island, 32

der Installateur (daiR in-shtahl-lah-tUR), plumber, 15

die Jacke (dee **yahk**-kuh), jacket, 7

der Jäger (daiR **yay**-geR), hunter, 24

der Jaguar (daiR **yah**-goo-ahR), jaguar, 20

die Jahreszeiten (dee **yah**-Res-tsigh-ten), seasons, 5

die Jalousien (dee yah-loo-**zee**-en), venetian blinds, 2

die Jeans (dee jeans), jeans, 7

der Jeep (daiR jeep), jeep, 16

das Joggen (dahs **johg**-gen), jogging, 18

der Jongleur (daiR johng-**lUR**), juggler, 21

jonglieren (johng-lee-**Ren**), juggle, 27

der Junge (daiR **yoon**-guh), boy, 9

das Juwel (dahs yoo-**vel**), jewel, 22

der Juwelier (daiR yoo-ve-**leeR**), jeweler, 15

der Kaffee (daiR kahf-**fay**), coffee, 10

der Käfig (daiR **kay**-fiH), cage, 21

kahl (kahl), bald, 12

der Kaktus (daiR **kahk**-toos), cactus, 1

das Kalb (dahs kahlb), calf, 9

der Kalender (daiR **kah**-len-deR), calendar, 1

kalt (kahlt), cold, 26

das Kamel (dahs kah-**mel**), camel, 20

die Kamera (dee **kah**-me-Rah), camera, 17, 21

der Kamin (daiR kah-**meen**), chimney, 2; fireplace, 2

der Kamm (daiR kahmm), comb, 12

der Kanal (daiR **Kah**-nahl), canal, 32

der Kanaldeckel (daiR kah-**nahl**-dek-kel), manhole cover, 8

der kandierte Apfel (daiR kahn-**deeR**-tuh **ahp**-fel), caramel apple, 21

das Känguruh (dahs **kayn**-goo-Roo), kangaroo, 20

die Kanone (dee kah-**noh**-nuh), cannon, 22

das Kanu (dahs kah-**noo**), canoe, 16

das Kap (dahs kahp), cape, 32

die Kapuze (dee kah-**poo**-tsuh), hood, 7

die Karotten (dee kah-**Roht**-ten), carrots, 6

der Karren (daiR **kahR**-Ren), cart, 24

die Karten (dee **kahR**-ten), cards, 4

die Kartenverkaufstelle (dee **kahR**-ten-faiR-kowf-shtel-luh), ticket booth, 21

die Kartoffelchips (dee kahR-**tohf**-fel-chips), potato chips, 6

die Kartoffeln (dee kahR-**tohf**-feln), potatoes, 6

der Käse (daiR **kay**-zuh), cheese, 6

die Kasse (dee **kahs**-suh), cash register, 6

die Kassette (dee kahs-**set**-tuh), cassette tape, 2

der Kassettenrecorder (daiR kahs-**set**-ten-Ray-kohR-deR), cassette player, 2

die Kassiererin (dee kahs-**see**-Re-Rin), cashier, teller, 6, 13

das Kätzchen (dahs **kayts**-Hen), kitten, 9

die Katze (dee **kaht**-tsuh), cat, 9

kaufen (**kow**-fen), buy, 27

der Kegel (daiR **kay**-gel), cone, 30

das Kegeln (dahs **kay**-geln), bowling, 18

die Kehrichtschaufel (dee **kay**-RiHt-show-fel), dustpan, 3

die Kekse (dee kayk-**zuh**), crackers, 6

der Kellner (daiR **kel**-neR), waiter, 10

die Kellnerin (dee **kel**-ne-Rin), waitress, 10

der Kerker (daiR **kaiR**-keR), dungeon, 25

die Kerze (dee **kaiR**-tsuh), candle, 10

der Ketchup (daiR **ketch**-oop), ketchup, 10

das Kettenhemd (dahs **ket**-ten-hemt), chain mail, 25

die Keule (dee **koy**-luh), club, 24

kicken (kik-**ken**), kick, 27

die Kiemen (dee **kee**-men), gills, 22

die Kinder (dee **kin**-deR), children, 19

der Kinderwagen (daiR **kin**-deR-vah-gen), baby carriage, 16

das Kinn (dahs kin), chin, 11

das Kino (dahs **kee**-noh), movie theater, 8

die Kirche (dee **keeR**-Huh), church, 8

die Kirsche (dee **keeR**-shuh), cherries, 6

die Kiste (dee **kis**-tuh), trunk, 4

die Klammern (dee **klahm**-meRn), braces, 11

die Klarinette (dee klah-Ri-**net**-tuh), clarinet, 19

das Klassenzimmer (dahs **klahs**-sen-tsim-meR), classroom, 1

das Klavier (dahs klah-**veeR**), piano, 19

der Klebstoff (daiR **klayb**-shtoff), glue, 1

das Kleid (dahs klight), dress, 7

der Kleiderbügel (daiR **kligh**-deR-bU-gel), hanger, 2

der Kleidersack (daiR **kligh**-deR-zahk), garment bag, 17

die Kleidung (dee **kligh**-doong), clothing, 7

klein (klighn), small, 26; short, 26

klettern (**klet**-teRn), climb, 27

das Knie (dahs knee), knee, 11

der Knochen (daiR **knoh**-Ken), bone, 24

der Knopf (daiR knohpf), button, 7

der Knoten (daiR **knoh**-ten), bun, 12; knot, 13

der Koch (daiR koK), cook, 15

kochen (ko-**Ken**), cook, 27

der Köcher (daiR **kER**-HeR), quiver, 25

der Koffer (daiR **kohf**-feR), suitcase, 17

der Kofferraum (daiR **kohf**-feR-Rowm), trunk, 14

der Kombiwagen (daiR **kohm**-bee-vah-gen), van, 16

der Komet (daiR koh-**mayt**), comet, 23

kommen (**kohm**-men), come, 27

der Kompaß (daiR **kohm**-pahs), compass, 32

der Komputer (daiR kohm-**pue**-teR), computer, 23

die Komputerprogrammiererin (dee kohm-**pue**-teR-pRoh-gRahm-**mee**-Re-Rin), computer programmer, 15

die Konfitüre (dee kohn-fi-**tU**-Ruh), jam, 10

der König (daiR **kER**-niH), king, 25

die Königin (dee **kER**-ni-gin), queen, 25

die Kontrolltafel (dee kohn-**tRohl**-tah-fel), control panel, 23

der Kontrollturm (daiR kohn-**tRohl**-tooRm), control tower, 17

der Kopf (daiR kohpf), head, 11

der Kopfhörer (daiR **kohpf**-hER-ReR), headset, 17

das Kopfkissen (dahs **kohpf**-kis-sen), pillow, 2

der Kopfstand (daiR **kohpf**-shtahnt), headstand, 21

der Kopilot (daiR **koh**-pee-loht), copilot, 17

die Koralle (dee koh-**Rahl**-luh), coral, 22

das Korallenriff (dahs koh-**Rahl**-len-Rif), coral reef, 22

der Korb (daiR kohRp), basket, 24

das Korbballspiel (dahs **kohRp**-bahl-shpeel), basketball, 18

das Kostüm (dahs koh-**stUm**), costume, 19

der Kotflügel (daiR **koht**-flU-gel), fender, 14

die Krabbe (die **kRahb**-buh), crab, 22

der Kragen (daiR **kRah**-gen), collar, 7

die Krallen (dee **kRahl**-len), claws, 20

der Kran (daiR kRahn), crane, 8

das Krankenhaus (dahs **kRahn**-ken-hows), hospital, 8

die Krankenschwester (dee **kRahn**-ken-shve-steR), nurse, 11

der Krankenwagen (daiR **kRahn**-ken-vah-gen), ambulance, 16

der Krater (daiR **kRah**-teR), crater, 23

das Kraut (dahs kRowt), cabbage, 6

die Krawatte (dee **kRah**-**vaht**-tuh), tie, 7

die Kreditkarte (dee kRe-**dit**-kahR-tuh), credit card, 13

die Kreide (dee **kRigh**-duh), chalk, 1

der Kreis (daiR kRighs), circle, 30

die Krone (dee **kRoh**-nuh), crown, 25

die Krücke (dee **kRUk**-kuh), crutch, 11

die Küche (dee **kU**-Huh), kitchen, 2, 3

der Kuchen (daiR **koo**-Ken), cake, 10

die Küchenmaschine (dee **kU**-Hen-mah-shee-nuh), word processor, 3

die Kugel (dee **koo**-gel), sphere, 30

der Kugelschreiber (daiR **koo**-gel-shRigh-beR), pen, 1

die Kuh (dee koo), cow, 9

der Kühlschrank (daiR **kUhl**-shRahnk), refrigerator, 3

die Kulisse (dee koo-**lis**-suh), scenery, 19

die Künstlerin (dee **kUnst**-le-Rin), artist, 15

kurz (kooRts), short, 12, 26

die Kusine (dee koo-**zee**-nuh), cousin, 29

das Labor (dahs lah-**bohR**), laboratory, 23

der Labormantel (daiR lah-**bohR**-mahn-tel), lab coat, 23

das Lächeln (dahs **lay**-Keln), smile, 11

lachen (**lah**-Hen), laugh, 27

das Lamm (dahs lahm), lamb, 9

die Lampe (dee **lahm**-puh), lamp, 2

das Land (dahs lahnt), country, 9

die Landkarte (dee **lahnt**-kahR-tuh), map, 1

das Landungsgerät (dahs **lahn**-doongs-ge-Rayt), landing capsule, 23

lang (lahng), long, 12, 26

der Langlauf (daiR **lahng**-lowf), cross-country skiing, 18

langsam (**lahng**-zahm), slow, 26

die Lanze (dee **lahn**-tsuh), lance, 25

der Lastwagen (daiR **lahst**-vah-gen), truck, 16

der Lastwagenfahrer (daiR **lahst**-vah-gen-fah-ReR), truck driver, 14

laufen (**low**-fen), run, 27

das Laufen (dahs **low**-fen), running, 18

der Lautsprecher (daiR **lowt**-shpRe-KeR), loudspeaker, 1

das Lebensmittelgeschäft (dahs **lay**-bens-mit-tel-ge-shayft), grocery store, 8

das Leder (dahs **lay**-deR), leather, 24

leer (laiR), empty, 26

der Lehm (daiR laym), clay, 24

lehren (**lay**-Ren), teach, 27

der Lehrer (daiR **lay**-ReR), teacher (male), 1

die Lehrerin (dee **lay**-Re-Rin), teacher (female), 1

das Lehrerpult (dahs **layR**-eR-poolt), teacher's desk, 1

leicht (lighHt), light, 26

die Leiter (dee **ligh**-teR), ladder, 23

das Lenkrad (dahs **laynk**-Raht), steering wheel, 14

die Lenkstange (dee **laynk**-shtahn-guh), handlebars, 14

der Leopard (daiR lay-oh-**pahRt**), leopard, 20

lesen (**lay**-zen), read, 27

der Leuchtturm (daiR **loyHt**-tooRm), lighthouse, 16

die Leute (die **loy**-tuh), people, 15

lila (**lee**-lah), purple, 28

die Limonade (dee li-moh-**nah**-duh), soft drink, 10

die Limone (dee li-**moh**-ne), lime, 6

das Lineal (dahs li-nay-**ahl**), ruler, 1

links (links), left, 26

die Lippen (dee **lip**-pen), lips, 11

der Lippenstift (daiR **lip**-pen-shtift), lipstick, 12

der Locher (daiR **loh**-KeR), hole punch, 1

der Lockenstab (daiR **lohk**-ken-shtahp), curling iron, 12

die Lockenwickel (dee **lohk**-ken-vik-kel), curlers, 12

lockig (**lok**-kiH), curly, 12

der Löffel (daiR **lERf**-fel), spoon, 10

der Löwe (daiR **lER**-vuh), lion, 20, 21

der Löwenbändiger (daiR **lER**-ven-bayn-di-geR), lion tamer, 21

der Luftballon (daiR **looft**-bahl-lohn), balloon, 21

das Luftschiff (dahs **looft**-shiff), blimp, 16

der Luftschlauch (daiR **looft**-shlowK), air hose, 14

der Lufttank (daiR **looft**-tahnk), oxygen tank, 22

die Luftverkehrskontrolleurin (dee **looft**-faiR-kaiRs-kohn-tRohl-lU-Rin), air-traffic controller, 17

die Luke (dee **loo**-kuh), porthole, 22

der Lumpen (daiR **loom**-pen), rag, 14

das Mädchen (dahs **mayt**-Hen), girl, 9

der Magnet (daiR mahg-**nayt**), magnet, 4

die Mahlzeiten (dee **mahl**-tsigh-ten), meals, 10

die Mähne (dee **mayh**-nuh), mane, 20

der Mais (daiR mighs), corn, 24

das Malbuch (dahs **mahl**-booK), coloring book, 4

malen (**mah**-len), paint, 27

das Mammut (dahs **mahm**-moot), mammoth, 24

die Manege (dee mah-**nay**-juh), ring, 21

der Mann (daiR mahn), man, 9

das Mannequin (dahs **mahn**-ne-kvin), model, 15

der Mantel (daiR **mahn**-tel), coat, 7

das Märchenschloß (dahs **mayR**-Hen-shlohs), make-believe castle, 25

das Maskara (dahs mahs-**kah**-Rah), mascara, 12

die Maske (dee **mahs**-kuh), mask, 19

der Matrose (daiR mah-**tRoh**-zuh), sailor, 15

der Matsch (daiR mahtsh), mud, 5

die Maus (dee mows), mouse, 9

die Mäusejagd (dee **moy**-ze-yahkt), mouse hunt, 26

der Mechaniker (daiR me-**kah**-ni-keR), mechanic, 14

die Medaille (dee me-**dahl**-yuh), medal, 18

die Medizin (dee me-di-**tseen**), medicine, 11

die Meerenge (dee **maiR**-en-guh), channel, 32

das Mehl (dahs mail), flour, 3

die Melone (dee me-**loh**-nuh), melon, 6

die Menschheitsgeschichte (dee **mensh**-hights-ge-shiH-tuh), human history, 24

das **Messer** (dahs **mes**-ser), knife, 10
der **Meteorschwarm** (daiR **may**-tay-ohR-shvahRm), meteor shower, 23
der **Metzger** (daiR **mets**-geR), butcher, 15
die **Metzgerei** (dee mets-ge-**Righ**), butcher shop, 8
das **Mikrofon** (dahs mee-kRoh-**fohn**), microphone, 19
das **Mikroskop** (dahs mee-kRoh-**skohp**), microscope, 23
der **Mikrowellenherd** (daiR mee-kRoh-**vel**-len-haiRt), microwave oven, 3
die **Milch** (dee milH), milk, 6
die **Milchstraße** (dee **milH**-shtRah-suh), galaxy, 23
eine **Milliarde** (**igh**-nuh mil-ly-**ahR**-duh), one billion, 31
eine **Million** (**igh**-nuh mil-ly-**ohn**), one million, 31
der **Minnesänger** (daiR **min**-ne-zayn-geR), minstrel, 25
das **Mittagessen** (dahs **mit**-tah-ges-sen), lunch, 10
mittel (**mit**-tel), medium, 26
der **Mixer** (daiR **mi**-kseR), electric mixer, 3
die **Modeschöpferin** (dee moh-duh-sh**ERp**-fe-Rin), fashion designer, 15
der **Mond** (daiR mohnt), moon, 23
das **Mondfahrzeug** (dahs **mohnt**-fahR-tsoyk), lunar rover, 23
das **Mondgestein** (dahs **mohnt**-ge-shtighn), moon rock, 23
der **Mop** (daiR mohp), mop, 3
der **Motor** (daiR moh-tohR), engine, 14, 17
das **Motorboot** (dahs moh-**tohR**-boht), motorboat, 16
das **Motorrad** (dahs moh-**tohR**-Raht), motorcycle, 16
das **Mühlespiel** (dahs **mUh**-luh-shpeel), checkers, 4
der **Mund** (daiR moont), mouth, 11
die **Münze** (dee m**Un**-tsuh), coin, 13
die **Murmeln** (dee **mooR**-meln), marbles, 4
die **Muschel** (dee **moo**-shel), clam, seashell, 22
das **Museum** (dahs moo-**zay**-oom), museum, 8
die **Mutter** (dee **moot**-teR), mother, 29
die **Mutti** (dee **moot**-tee), mom, 29

die **Nabe** (dee **nah**-buh), hubcap, 14
die **Nacht** (dee nahKt), night, 21
der **Nachttisch** (der **nahKt**-tish), night table, 2
der **Nagel** (der **nah**-gel), nail, 3
die **Nagelfeile** (dee **nah**-gel-pfigh-luh), nail file, 12
der **Nagellack** (daiR **nah**-gel-lahk), nail polish, 12
die **Nagelschere** (dee **nah**-gel-shai-Ruh), nail clippers, 12
nah (nah), near, 26
die **Nähmaschine** (dee **nay**-mah-shee-nuh), sewing machine, 19
naß (nahs), wet, 26
die **Nase** (dee **nah**-zuh), nose, 11
das **Nashorn** (dahs **nahs**-hohRn), rhinoceros, 20
der **Naturwissenschaftler** (daiR nah-**tooR**-vis-sen-shahft-leR), scientist, 23
der **Navigationsoffizier** (deR nah-vi-gah-tsi-**ohns**-ohf-fi-tseeR), navigator, 17
der **Nebel** (daiR **nay**-bel), fog, 5
der **Nebelfleck** (daiR **nay**-bel-flek), nebula, 23
neben (**nay**-ben), next to, 26
das **Netz** (dahs nets), net, 18
neu (noy), new, 26
neun (noyn), nine, 31
neunt- (noynt), ninth, 31

neunundachtzig (noyn-oont-**ahKt**-tsiH), eighty-nine, 31
neununddreißig (noyn-oont-**dRigh**-tsiH), thirty-nine, 31
neunundfünfzig (noyn-oont-**fUnf**-tsiH), fifty-nine, 31
neunundneunzig (noyn-oont-**noyn**-tsiH), ninety-nine, 31
neunundsechzig (noyn-oont-**zeK**-tsiH), sixty-nine, 31
neunundsiebzig (noyn-oont-**zeep**-tsiH), seventy-nine, 31
neunundvierzig (noyn-oont-**feeR**-tsiH), forty-nine, 31
neunundzwanzig (noyn-oont-tsvahn-tsiH), twenty-nine, 31
neunzehn (**noyn**-tsayhn), nineteen, 31
neunzig (**noyn**-tsiH), ninety, 31
das **Niesen** (dahs **nee**-zen), sneeze, 11
Nordamerika (**nohRd**-ah-may-Ri-kah), North America, 32
der **Norden** (dahs **nohR**-den), north, 32
das **nördliche Eismeer** (dahs n**ERd**-li-Huh ighs-maiR), Arctic Ocean, 32
der **Nordosten** (daiR **nohRd**-oh-sten), northeast, 32
der **Nordpol** (daiR **nohR**-dpohl), North Pole, 32
der **Nordwesten** (daiR **nohRd**-ves-ten), northwest, 32
die **Noten** (dee **noh**-ten), sheet music, 19
der **Notizblock** (daiR noh-**teets**-blohk), notepad, 13
die **Nudeln** (dee **noo**-deln), noodles, 10
null (nool), zero, 31
die **Nummern** (dee **noom**-meRn), numbers, 1, 31
die **Nüsse** (dee n**Us**-suh), nuts, 6

die **Oase** (dee oh-**ah**-zuh), oasis, 32
oben (**oh**-ben), up, 26
die **Oberseite** (dee **oh**-beR-zigh-tuh), top, 26
das **Obst** (dahs ohbst), fruit, 6
der **Obstkuchen** (daiR **ohbst**-koo-Ken), pie, 6
offen (**ohf**-fen), open, 26
öffnen (**ERf**-nen), open, 27
das **Ohr** (dahs ohR), ear, 11
die **Ohrenschützer** (dee **oh**-Ren-shUt-tseR), earmuffs, 7
der **Ohrring** (daiR **ohR**-Ring), earring, 7
das **Öl** (dahs ERl), oil, 14
die **Oma** (dee **oh**-mah), grandma, 29
das **Omelett** (dahs ohm-**let**), omelet, 10
der **Onkel** (daiR **ohn**-kel), uncle, 29
der **Opa** (daiR **oh**-pah), grandpa, 29
die **Optikerin** (dee **ohp**-ti-ke-Rin), optician, 15
orange (oh-**Rahn**-juh), orange, 28
die **Orange** (dee oh-**Rahn**-juh), orange, 6
das **Orchester** (dahs ohR-**Ke**-steR), band, 21; orchestra, 19
der **Orchesterraum** (daiR ohR-**Ke**-steR-Rowm), orchestra pit, 19
die **Ordnungszahlen** (dee **ohRd** noongs tsah len), ordinal numbers, 31
der **Osten** (daiR **oh**-sten), east, 32
das **Oval** (dahs oh-**vahl**), oval, 30
der **Overall** (daiR **oh**-veR-ahl), coveralls, 14
der **Ozean** (daiR **oh**-tsee-ahn), ocean, 22

das **Paket** (dahs pah-**kayt**), package, 13
das **Paketklebeband** (dahs pah-**kayt**-klay-buh-bahnt), packing tape, 13
die **Pampelmuse** (dee **pahm**-pel-moo-zuh), grapefruit, 6
der **Panda** (daiR **pahn**-dah), panda, 20

die **Panne** (dee **pahn**-nuh), flat tire, 14
der **Papagei** (daiR pah-pah-**gigh**), parrot, 20
das **Papier** (dahs pah-**peeR**), paper, 1
der **Papierkorb** (daiR pah-**peeR**-kohRp), wastebasket, 1
die **Papiertücher** (dee pah-**peeR**-tU-KeR), paper towels, 3
der **Park** (daiR pahRk), park, 8
der **Parkplatz** (daiR **pahRk**-plahtz), parking lot, 8
die **Parkuhr** (dee **pahRk**-ooR), parking meter, 8
der **Paß** (daiR pahs), passport, 17
der **Passagier** (daiR pahs-sah-**jeeR**), passenger, 17
der **Passagierdampfer** (daiR pahs-sah-**jeeR**-dahmp-feR), cruise ship, 16
der **Patient** (daiR pah-tsee-**ent**), patient, 11
der **Pazifik** (daiR pah-**tsi**-fik), Pacific Ocean, 32
das **Pedal** (dahs pe-**dahl**), pedal, 14
die **Peitsche** (dee **pight**-shuh), whip, 21
der **Pelz** (daiR pelts), fur, 24
die **Perücke** (dee pe-**Ruk**-kuh), wig, 19
die **Pfanne** (dee **pfahn**-nuh), pan, 3
der **Pfau** (daiR pfow), peacock, 20
der **Pfeffer** (daiR **pfef**-feR), pepper, 10
die **Pfeife** (dee **pfigh**-fuh), whistle, 4
der **Pfeil** (daiR pfighl), arrow, 25
die **Pfeilspitze** (dee **pfighl**-shpit-tsuh), arrowhead, 24
das **Pferd** (dahs pfaiRd), horse, 9
das **Pferderennen** (dahs **pfaiR**-duh-Ren-nen), horse racing, 18
der **Pferdeschwanz** (daiR **pfaiR**-duh-shvahnts), ponytail, 12
der **Pfirsich** (daiR **pfeeR**-ziH), peach, 6
die **Pflanze** (dee **pflahn**-tsuh), plant, 1
das **Pflaster** (dahs **pflah**-steR), bandage, 11
die **Pfütze** (dee **pfUt**-tsuh), puddle, 5
die **Photographie** (dee foh-toh-gRah-**fee**), photograph, 4
das **Picknick** (dahs **pick**-nick), picnic, 9
der **Pier** (daiR peeR), dock, 16
die **Pille** (dee **pil**-luh), pill, 11
der **Pilot** (daiR pee-**loht**), pilot, 17
der **Pilz** (daiR pilts), mushroom, 10
der **Pinguin** (daiR pin-gu-**een**), penguin, 20
der **Pinsel** (daiR **pin**-zel), paintbrush, 1
das **Plakat** (dahs plah-**kaht**), poster, 2
der **Planet** (daiR plah-**nayt**), planet, 23
der **Plattenspieler** (daiR **plaht**-ten-shpee-leR), record player, 2
der **Platz** (daiR plahts), square, 8
die **Plätzchen** (dee **playts**-Hen), cookies, 6
das **Polizeiauto** (dahs poh-li-**tsigh**-ow-toh), police car, 16
die **Polizeiwache** (dee poh-li-**tsigh**-vah-Kuh), police station, 8
der **Polizist** (daiR poh-li-**tsist**), policeman, 15
die **Polizistin** (dee poh-li-**tsi**-stin), policewoman, 15
die **Pommes frites** (dee pohm fRits), french fries, 10
der **Pony** (daiR **poh**-nee), bangs, 12
das **Popkorn** (dahs **pohp**-kohRn), popcorn, 21
der **Portier** (daiR pohR-**teeR**), doorman, 15
die **Posaune** (dee poh-**zow**-nuh), trombone, 19
das **Postamt** (dahs **pohst**-ahmt), post office, 13
der **Postbeamte** (daiR **pohst**-be-ahm-tuh), postal worker, 13
das **Postfach** (dahs **pohst**-fahK), post-office box, 13
die **Postkarte** (dee **pohst**-kahR-tuh), postcard, 13
die **Postleitzahl** (dee **pohst**-light-tsahl), zip code, 13
der **Poststempel** (daiR **pohst**-shtem-pel), postmark, 13

die **Präpositionen** (dee pRay-poh-zi-tsee-**oh**-nen), prepositions, 26

der **Preis** (daiR pRighs), price, 6

der **Prinz** (daiR pRints), prince, 25

die **Prinzessin** (dee pRin-**tses**-sin), princess, 25

der **Programmleiter** (daiR pRoh-**gRahm**-ligh-teR), master of ceremonies, 19

der **Propeller** (daiR proh-**pel**-leR), propeller, 17

der **Puder** (daiR poo-deR), powder, 12

der **Pullover** (daiR pool-oh-**veR**), sweater, 7

das **Pult** (dahs poolt), pupil desk, 1

die **Puppe** (dee **poop**-puh), doll, 4

das **Puppenhaus** (dahs **poop**-pen-hows), dollhouse, 4

der **Purzelbaum** (daiR **pooR**-tsel-bowm), somersault, 21

das **Puzzle** (dahs **pooz**-zel), jigsaw puzzle, 4

die **Qualle** (dee **kvahl**-luh), jellyfish, 22

das **Rad** (dahs Raht), cartwheel, 21; wheel, 24

der **Radarschirm** (daiR Rah-**dahR**-sheeRm), radar screen, 17

das **Radfahren** (dahs **Raht**-fah-Ren), cycling, 18

der **Radiergummi** (daiR Rah-**deeR**-goom-mee), eraser, 1

das **Radio** (dahs **Rah**-dee-oh), radio, 2

die **Rakete** (dee Rah-**kay**-tuh), rocket, 23

der **Rasenmäher** (daiR **Rah**-zen-may-eR), lawn mower, 5

der **Rasensprenger** (daiR **Rah**-zen-shpRen-geR), sprinkler, 5

die **Rasiercreme** (dee Rah-**zeeR**-kRaym), shaving cream, 12

das **Rasiermesser** (dahs Rah-**zeeR**-mes-seR), razor, 12

die **Ratte** (dee **Raht**-tuh), rat, 25

der **Rauch** (daiR RowK), smoke, 9

der **Raumanzug** (daiR **Rowm**-ahn-tsook), space suit, 23

die **Raumfähre** (dee **Rowm**-fay-ruh), space shuttle, 23

der **Raumhelm** (daiR **Rowm**-helm), space helmet, 23

das **Raumschiff** (dahs **Rowm**-shif), spaceship, 23

die **Raumstation** (dee **Rowm**-shtah-tsee-ohn), space station, 23

die **Raumwanderung** (dee **Rowm**-vahn-de-Roong), space walk, 23

das **Reagenzglas** (dahs Ray-ah-**gents**-glahs), test tube, 23

der **Rechen** (daiR **Re**-Hen), rake, 5

die **Rechenaufgabe** (dee **Re**-Hen-owf-gah-buh), arithmetic problem, 1

der **Rechner** (daiR **ReH**-neR), calculator, 1

rechts (ReHts), right, 26

das **Rechteck** (dahs **ReH**-tek), rectangle, 30

die **Rechtsanwältin** (dee **ReHts**-ahn-vayl-tin), lawyer, 15

reden (**Ray**-den), talk, 27

das **Regal** (dahs Ray-**gahl**), shelf, 2

der **Regen** (daiR **Ray**-gen), rain, 5

der **Regenbogen** (daiR **Ray**-gen-boh-gen), rainbow, 5

der **Regenmantel** (daiR **Ray**-gen-mahn-tel), raincoat, 7

der **Regenschirm** (daiR **Ray**-gen-sheeRm), umbrella, 4, 7

der **Regentropfen** (daiR **Ray**-gen-tRohp-fen), raindrop, 5

das **Reh** (dahs Ray), deer, 20

der **Reifen** (daiR **Righ**-fen), hoop, 21; tire, 14

der **Reis** (daiR Righs), rice, 10

der **Reißverschluß** (daiR **Righs**-faiR-schloos), zipper, 7

das **Reiten** (dahs **Righ**-ten), horseback riding, 18

das **Rennauto** (dahs **Ren**-ow-toh), race car, 14

reparieren (Re-pah-**Ree**-Ren), fix, 27

der **Reporter** (daiR Ray-**pohR**-teR), reporter, 15

das **Restaurant** (dahs Re-stow-**Rahn**), restaurant, 8, 10

die **Rettungsleiter** (dee **Ret**-toongs-ligh-teR), fire escape, 8

die **Richterin** (dee **RiH**-te-Rin), judge, 15

der **Riese** (daiR **Ree**-zuh), giant, 25

der **Ring** (daiR Ring), ring, 7

das **Ringen** (dahs **Rin**-gen), wrestling, 18

der **Ritter** (daiR **Rit**-teR), knight, 25

die **Robbe** (dee **Rohb**-buh), seal, 20

der **Roboter** (daiR **Roh**-boh-teR), robot, 23

der **Rock** (daiR Rohk), skirt, 7

der **Roller** (daiR **Rohl**-leR), scooter, 16

die **Rollschuhe** (dee **Rohl**-shoo-huh), roller skates, 16

der **Rollstuhl** (daiR **Rohl**-shtool), wheelchair, 11

die **Rolltreppe** (dee **Rohl**-tRep-puh), escalator, 17

die **Röntgenstrahlen** (dee **RERnt**-gen-shtRah-len), X ray, 11

rosa (**Roh**-zah), pink, 28

rot (Roht), red, 12, 28

der **Rücken** (daiR **RUk**-ken), back, 11

der **Rucksack** (daiR **Rook**-zahk), backpack, 7

der **Rücksitz** (daiR **RUk**-zits), backseat, 14

der **Rückspiegel** (daiR **RUk**-shpee-gel), rearview mirror, 14

die **Rückstrahler** (dee **RUk**-shtRah-leR), reflectors, 14

das **Ruder** (dahs **Roo**-deR), oar, 16

das **Ruderboot** (dahs **Roo**-deR-boht), rowboat, 16

der **Rüssel** (daiR **RUs**-sel), trunk, 24

die **Rüstung** (dee **RU**-stoong), armor, 25

die **Rutschbahn** (dee **Rootsh**-bahn), slide, 8

der **Säbelzahntiger** (daiR **zay**-bel-tsahn-tee-geR), saber-toothed tiger, 24

die **Säge** (dee **zay**-guh), saw, 3

die **Sahne** (dee **zah**-nuh), cream, 10

die **Saiten** (dee **zigh**-ten), strings, 19

der **Salat** (daiR zah-**laht**), lettuce, 6; salad, 10

das **Salz** (dahs sahlts), salt, 10

der **Sand** (daiR sahnt), sand, 22

die **Sandalen** (dee sahn-**dah**-len), sandals, 7

der **Sandkasten** (daiR **sahnt**-kahs-ten), sandbox, 8

das **Sandpapier** (dahs **sahnt**-pah-peeR), sandpaper, 3

der **Sänger** (daiR **zayn**-geR), singer, 19

der **Sattel** (daiR **zaht**-tel), saddle, 25

die **sattellose Reiterin** (dee **saht**-tel-loh-zuh **Righ**-te-Rin), bareback rider, 21

sauber (**zow**-beR), clean, 26

das **Saxophon** (dahs **zahks**-oh-fohn), saxophone, 19

das **Schachspiel** (dahs **shahK**-shpeel), chess, 4

die **Schachtel** (dee **shahK**-tel), box, 4

das **Schaf** (dahs shahf), sheep, 9

die **Schallplatte** (dee **shahl**-plaht-tuh), record, 2

der **Schalter** (daiR **shahl**-teR), ticket counter, 17

scharf (shahRf), sharp, 26

der **Schatten** (daiR **shaht**-ten), shadow, 9

der **Schatz** (daiR shahts), treasure, 22

die **Schatzkiste** (dee **shahts**-kis-tuh), treasure chest, 22

die **Schaufel** (dee **show**-fel), shovel, 5

die **Schaukel** (dee **show**-kel), swings, 8

das **Schaukelpferd** (dahs **show**-kel-pfaiRd), rocking horse, 4

der **Schaukelstuhl** (daiR **show**-kel-shtool), rocking chair, 2, 4

der **Schaum** (daiR showm), mousse, 12; suds, 12

der **Schauspieler** (daiR **show**-shpee-leR), actor, 19

die **Schauspielerin** (dee **show**-shpee-le-Rin), actress, 19

der **Scheck** (daiR shek), check, 13

das **Scheckbuch** (dahs **shek**-booK), checkbook, 13

die **Scheibenwischer** (dee **shigh**-ben-vi-sheR), windshield wipers, 14

der **Schein** (daiR shighn), bill, 13

der **Scheinwerfer** (daiR **shighn**-vaiR-feR), headlight, 14; spotlight, 19

der **Scheitel** (daiR **shigh**-tel), part, 12

die **Schere** (dee **she**-Ruh), scissors, 1, 12

die **Scheune** (dee **shoy**-nuh), barn, 9

das **Schiebedach** (dahs **shee**-be-dahK), sunroof, 14

schieben (**shee**-ben), push, 27

der **Schiedsrichter** (daiR **sheeds**-RiH-teR), referee, umpire, 18

die **Schier** (dee **shee**-eer), skis, 18

schifahren (**shee**-fah-Ren), ski, 27

der **Schiffbruch** (daiR **shiff**-bRooH), shipwreck, 22

der **Schild** (daiR shilt), shield, 25

die **Schildkröte** (dee **shilt**-kRER-tuh), turtle, 20

der **Schinken** (daiR **shin**-ken), ham, 10

der **Schlafanzug** (daiR **shlahf**-ahn-tsook), pajamas, 7

schlafen (**shlah**-fen), sleep, 27

der **Schlafsack** (daiR **shlahf**-zahk), sleeping bag, 9

das **Schlafzimmer** (dahs **shlahf**-tsim-meR), bedroom, 2

der **Schläger** (daiR **shlay**-geR), racket, 18

die **Schlange** (dee **shlahn**-guh), snake, 20

die **Schleife** (dee **shligh**-fuh), bow, 13

der **Schlepper** (daiR **shlep**-peR), tugboat, 16

die **Schlinge** (dee **shlin**-guh), sling, 11

der **Schlitten** (daiR **shlit**-ten), sled, 5

die **Schlittschuhe** (dee **shlit**-shoo-uh), skates, 18

das **Schloß** (dahs shlohs), castle, 25; lock, 13

der **Schlüssel** (daiR **shlUs**-sel), key, 13

schmal (shmahl), narrow, 26

der **Schmetterling** (daiR **shmet**-teR-ling), butterfly, 5

die **Schmiede** (dee **shmee**-duh), forge, 25

die **Schminke** (dee **shmin**-kuh), makeup, 19

der **Schmutz** (daiR shmoots), dirt, 9

schmutzig (**shmoot**-tsiH), dirty, 26

der **Schnabel** (daiR **shnah**-bel), beak, 20

die **Schnalle** (dee **shnahl**-luh), buckle, 7

der **Schnee** (daiR shnay), snow, 5

der **Schneeball** (daiR **shnay**-bahl), snowball, 5

die **Schneeflocke** (dee **shnay**-flohk-kuh), snowflake, 5

der **Schneemann** (daiR **shnay**-mahn), snowman, 5

das **Schneemobil** (dahs **shnay**-moh-beel), snowmobile, 5

der **Schneepflug** (daiR **shnay**-pflook), snowplow, 5

der **Schneesturm** (daiR **shnay**-shtooRm), snowstorm, 5

schneiden (**shnigh**-den), cut, 27

der **Schneider** (daiR **shnigh**-deR), tailor, 15

schnell (shnel), fast, 26

der **Schnorchel** (daiR **shnohR**-Hel), snorkel, 22

die **Schnur** (dee shnooR), string, 4, 13

der **Schnurrbart** (daiR **shnooR**-bahRt), mustache, 12

der Schnürsenkel (daiR **shnUR**-zenk-el), shoelace, 7

die Schokolade (dee shoh-koh-**lah**-duh), chocolate, 6

der Schornstein (daiR **shohRn**-shtighn), smokestack, 8

die Schraube (dee **shRow**-buh), screw, 3

der Schraubenschlüssel (daiR **shRow**-ben-shlUs-sel), wrench, 3

der Schraubenzieher (daiR **shRow**-ben-tsee-eR), screwdriver, 3

schreiben (**shRigh**-ben), write, 27

die Schreibmaschine (dee **schrighb**-mah-shee-nuh), typewriter, 13

der Schreiner (daiR **shRigh**-neR), carpenter, 15

die Schublade (dee **shoop**-lah-duh), drawer, 3

die Schuhe (dee **shoo**-uh), shoes, 7

der Schulbus (daiR **school**-boos), school bus, 16

die Schule (dee **shoo**-luh), school, 8

der Schüler (daiR **shU**-leR), student (male), 1

die Schülerin (dee **shU**-le-Rin), student (female), 1

die Schulter (dee **shool**-teR), shoulder, 11

die Schuppen (dee **shoop**-pen), scales, 22

die Schürze (dee **shooR**-tsuh), apron, 3

die Schüssel (dee **shUs**-sel), bowl, 10

die Schutzbrille (dee **shoots**-bRil-luh), goggles, 18

die Schutzhaube (dee **shoots**-how-buh), hood, 14

der Schwamm (daiR shvahm), eraser (chalkboard), 1; sponge, 3

der Schwan (daiR shvahn), swan, 20

der Schwanz (daiR shvahnts), tail, 20

schwarz (shvahRts), black, 12, 28

das Schwein (dahs shvighn), pig, 9

schwer (shvaiR), heavy, 26

das Schwert (dahs shvaiRt), sword, 25

der Schwertfisch (daiR **shvaiRt**-fish), swordfish, 22

die Schwester (dee **shves**-teR), sister, 29

schwierig (**shvee**-RiH), difficult, 26

das Schwimmbad (dahs **shvim**-bahd), swimming pool, 18

schwimmen (**shvim**-men), swim, 27

das Schwimmen (dahs **shvim**-men), swimming, 18

die Schwimmflosse (dee **shvim**-flohs-suh), flipper, 22

sechs (zeKs), six, 31

sechst- (zeKst), sixth, 31

sechsundachtzig (zeKs-oont-**ahKt**-tsiH), eighty-six, 31

sechsunddreißig (zeKs-oont-**dRigh**-tsiH), thirty-six, 31

sechsundfünfzig (zeKs-oont-**fUnf**-tsiH), fifty-six, 31

sechsundneunzig (zeKs-oont-**noyn**-tsiH), ninety-six, 31

sechsundsechzig (zeKs-oont-**zeK**-tsiH), sixty-six, 31

sechsundsiebzig (zeKs-oont-**zeep**-tsiH), seventy six, 31

sechsundvierzig (zeKs-oont-**feeR**-tsiH), forty-six, 31

sechsundzwanzig (zeKs-oont-**tsvahn**-tsiH), twenty-six, 31

sechzehn (**zeK**-tsayn), sixteen, 31

sechzig (**zeK**-tsiH), sixty, 31

der See (daiR zay), lake, 32

die See (dee zay), sea, 32

der Seeigel (daiR **zay**-ee-gel), sea urchin, 22

das Seepferdchen (dahs **zay**-pfaiRd-Hen), sea horse, 22

der Seepolyp (daiR **zay**-poh-lyp), octopus, 22

die Seeschildkröte (dee **zay**-shilt-kRER-tuh), sea turtle, 22

der Seestern (daiR **zay**-shtaiRn), starfish, 22

der Seetang (daiR **zay**-tahng), seaweed, 22

das Segel (dahs **zay**-gel), sail, 16

das Segelboot (dahs **zay**-gel-boht), sailboat, 16

das Segeln (dahs **zay**-geln), sailing, 18

die Seife (die **zigh**-fuh), soap, 6

das Seil (dahs zighl), rope, 19, 21

die Seilleiter (dee **zighl**-ligh-teR), rope ladder, 21

die Sekretärin (dee zek-Re-**tai**-Rin), secretary, 15

der Sellerie (daiR **zel**-le-Ree), celery, 10

der Senf (daiR zenf), mustard, 10

die Serviette (dee zeR-vee-**et**-tuh), napkin, 10

der Sessel (daiR **zes**-sel), armchair, 2

das Shampoo (dahs **shahm**-poo), shampoo, 12

die Shorts (dee shohRts), shorts, 7

sich hinsetzen (ziH **hin**-zet-tsen), sit down, 27

die Sicherheitskontrolle (dee **zi**-HeR-hights-kohn-tRoh-luh), metal detector, 17

das Sicherheitsnetz (dahs **zi**-HeR-hights-netz), safety net, 21

sieben (**zee**-ben), seven, 31

siebenundachtzig (zee-ben-oont-**ahKt**-tsiH), eighty-seven, 31

siebenunddreißig (zee-ben-oont-**dRigh**-tsiH), thirty-seven, 31

siebenundfünfzig (zee-ben-oont-**fUnf**-tsiH), fifty-seven, 31

siebenundneunzig (zee-ben-oont-**noyn**-tsiH), ninety-seven, 31

siebenundsechzig (zee-ben-oont-**zeK**-tsiH), sixty-seven, 31

siebenundsiebzig (zee-ben-oont-**zeep**-tsiH), seventy-seven, 31

siebenundvierzig (zee-ben-oont-**feeR**-tsiH), forty-seven, 31

siebenundzwanzig (zee-been-oont-**tsvahn**-tsiH), twenty-seven, 31

siebt- (zeept), seventh, 31

siebzehn (**zeep**-tsayhn), seventeen, 31

siebzig (**zeep**-tsiH), seventy, 31

das Silber (dahs **zil**-beR), silver, 22

silbern (**zil**-beRn), silver, 28

singen (**zin**-gen), sing, 27

der Sitz (daiR zits), seat, 17

der Sitzgurt (daiR **zits**-gooRt), seat belt, 14

das Skateboard (dahs **skate**-boaRd), skateboard, 16

das Skelett (dahs ske-**let**), skeleton, 24

der Smoking (daiR **smoh**-king), tuxedo, 4

die Socken (dee **zohk**-ken), socks, 7

das Sofa (dahs **zoh**-fah), sofa, 2

der Sohn (daiR zohn), son, 29

der Sommer (dair **sohm**-meR), summer, 5

die Sommersprossen (dee **sohm**-meR-shpRohs-sen), freckles, 12

die Sonne (dee **zohn**-nuh), sun, 23

die Sonnenbrille (dee **zohn**-nen-bRil-luh), sunglasses, 7

das Sonnensystem (dahs **zohn**-nen-zys-taym), solar system, 23

die Sonnenzellen (dee **zohn**-nen-tsel-len), solar cells, 23

der Spachtel (daiR **shpahK**-tel), spatula, 3

das Sparschwein (dahs **shpahR**-shvighn), piggy bank, 13

der Speer (daiR shpayR), spear, 24

die Speichen (dee **shpigh**-Hen), spokes, 14

die Speisekarte (die **shpigh**-zuh-kahR-tuh), menu, 10

der Spiegel (daiR **shpee**-gel), mirror, 2

das Spiel (dahs shpeel), game, 4

die Spieldose (dee **shpeel**-doh-zuh), music box, 4

spielen (**shpee**-len), play (a game), 27; play (an instrument), 27

das Spielgerät (dahs **shpeel**-ge-Rayt), jungle gym, 8

der Spielplatz (daiR **shpeel**-plahts), playground, 8

die Spielsachen (dee **shpeel**-zah-Ken), toys, 4

der Spielwarenladen (daiR **shpeel**-vah-Ren-lah-den), toy store, 8

die Spielzeugsoldaten (daiR **shpeel**-tsoyk-zohl-dah-ten), toy soldiers, 4

der Spinat (daiR shpi-**naht**), spinach, 6

die Spinne (dee **shpin**-nuh), spider, 25

das Spinnennetz (dahs **shpin**-nen-nets) spiderweb, 25

das Spinnrad (dahs **shpin**-Raht), spinning wheel, 4

die Spinnwebe (dee **shpin**-vay-buh), cobweb, 4

der Spitzer (daiR **shpit**-tseR), pencil sharpener, 1

der Sport (daiR shpohRt), sports, 18

der Sportler (daiR **shpohRt**-leR), athlete, 15

der Sportwagen (daiR **shpohRt**-vah-gen), stroller, 16

springen (**shpRin**-gen), jump, 27

das Springseil (dahs **shpRing**-zighl), jump rope, 4

die Spritze (dee **shpRit**-tsuh), hypodermic needle, 11

das Spülbecken (dahs **shpUl**-bek-ken), sink, 3

die Spülmaschine (dee **shpUl**-mah-shee-nuh), dishwasher, 3

der Stab (daiR shtahp), baton, 21

die Stadt (dee shtaht), city, 8

die Staffelei (dee shtahf-fe-**ligh**), easel, 1

der Stall (daiR shtahl), stable, 25

der Stammbaum (daiR **shtahm**-bowm), family tree, 29

die Startbahn (dee **shtaRt**-bahn), runway, 17

die Statue (dee shtah-**too**-huh), statue, 8

der Staub (daiR shtowp) dust, 4

der Staubsauger (daiR **shtowp**-sow-geR), vacuum cleaner, 3

das Steak (dahs shtayk), steak, 10

der Stechrochen (daiR **shteH**-Roh-Ken), stingray, 22

die Steckdose (dee **shtek**-doh-zuh), electrical outlet, 3

der Steigbügel (daiR **shtighk**-bU-gel), stirrup, 25

die Stelzen (dee **shtel**-tsen), stilts, 21

der Stempel (daiR **shtem**-pel), rubber stamp, 13

das Stempelkissen (dahs **shtem**-pel-kis-sen), ink pad, 13

der Stengel (daiR **sten**-gel), stem, 5

das Sternbild (dahs **shtaiRn**-bilt), constellation, 23

die Sterne (dee **shtaiR**-nuh), stars, 23

das Stethoskop (dahs shtay-toh-**skohp**), stethoscope, 11

die Stiefel (dee **shtee**-fel), boots, 7

die Stirn (dee shteeRn), forehead, 11

der Stock (daiR shtohk), cane, 11; stick, 24

das Stopschild (dahs **shtohp**-shilt), stop sign, 16

der Stoßzahn (daiR **shtohs**-tsahn), tusk, 24

der Strand (daiR shtRahnt), beach, 8

die Straße (dee **shtRah**-suh), street, 16

die Straßenkreuzung (dee **shtRah**-sen-kroy-tsoonk), intersection, 16

der Strauß (daiR shtRows), ostrich, 20

die Streichhölzer (dee **shtRighH**-hERl-tseR), matches, 5

die Streifen (dee **shtRigh**-fen), stripes, 20

die **Strickmütze** (dee **shtRik**-mUt-tsuh), cap, 7
die **Stricknadeln** (dee **shtRik**-nah-deln), knitting needles, 4
die **Strumpfhose** (dee **shtRoompf**-hoh-zuh), tights, 7
der **Stuhl** (daiR shtoohl), chair, 3
stumpf (shtoompf), dull, 26
die **Stützräder** (dee **shtUts** -Ray-deR), training wheels, 14
suchen (**zoo**-Hen), look for, 27
Südamerika (**zUd**-ah-may-Ri-kah), South America, 32
der **Süden** (daiR **zU**-den), south, 32
der **Südosten** (daiR **zUd-oh**-sten), southeast, 32
der **Südpol** (daiR **zUd**-pohl), South Pole, 32
der **Südwesten** (daiR **zUd-ves**-ten), southwest, 32
der **Supermarkt** (daiR **zoo**-peR-mahRkt), supermarket, 6
die **Suppe** (dee **zoop**-puh), soup, 10
die **Süßigkeiten** (dee **zUs**-siK-kigh-ten), candy, 6
das **Sweatshirt** (dahs **svet**-shiRt), sweatshirt, 7

das **Tablett** (dahs tah-**blet**), tray, 10
die **Tankstelle** (dee **tahnk**-shtel-luh), gas station, 14
der **Tankverschluß** (daiR **tahnk**-faiR-shloos), gas cap, 14
der **Tankwagen** (daiR **tahnk**-vah-gen), tank truck, 14
die **Tante** (dee **tahn**-tuh), aunt, 29
tanzen (**tahn**-tsen), dance, 27
die **Tänzerin** (dee **tayn**-tse-Rin), dancer, 19
das **Tanzkostüm** (dahs **tahnts**-koh-stUm), tutu, 19
die **Tasche** (dee **tah**-shuh), pocket, 7
die **Taschenlampe** (dee **tah**-shen-lahm-puh), flashlight, 3
das **Taschentuch** (dahs **tah**-shen-tooK), handkerchief, 7
die **Tasse** (dee **tahs**-suh), cup, 10
die **Tätigkeitswörter** (dee **tayt**-iH-kights-wERR-teR), action words, 27
die **Tatze** (dee **taht**-tsuh), paw, 20
tauchen (**tow**-Ken), dive, 27
das **Tauchen** (dahs **tow**-Ken), diving, 18
der **Taucher** (daiR **tow**-KeR), scuba diver, 22
die **Tauchermaske** (dee **tow**-KeR-mahs-kuh), mask, 22
tausend (**tow**-zent), one thousand, 31
das **Taxi** (dahs **tah**-ksee), taxi, 16
der **Taxifahrer** (daiR **tah**-ksee-fah-ReR), taxi driver, 15
der **Teddybär** (daiR **ted**-dy-bayR), teddy bear, 4
der **Tee** (daiR tay), tea, 10
der **Teich** (daiR tighH), pond, 9
das **Telefon** (dahs te-le-**fohn**), telephone, 2
die **Telefonzelle** (dee te-le-**fohn**-tsel-luh), phone booth, 13
der **Teller** (daiR **tel**-leR), plate, 10
der **Tennisschläger** (daiR **ten**-nis-shlay-geR), tennis racket, 17
das **Tennisspiel** (dahs **ten**-nis-shpeel), tennis, 18
der **Teppich** (daiR **tep**-piH), carpet, 2; rug, 1
der **Tesafilm** (daiR **tay**-zah-film), cellophane tape, 1
die **Theke** (dee **tay**-kuh), counter, 3
das **Thermometer** (dahs taiR-moh-**may**-teR), thermometer, 11
der **Thron** (daiR tRohn), throne, 25
die **Tiefkühlkost** (dee **teef**-kUhl-kohst), frozen dinner, 6

die **Tiefkühltruhe** (dee **teef**-kUhl-tRoo-uh), freezer, 3
die **Tierärztin** (dee **teeR**-ayRts-tin), veterinarian, 15
die **Tiere** (dee **tee**-Ruh), animals, 20
der **Tierpfleger** (daiR **teeR**-pflay-geR), zookeeper, 20
der **Tiger** (daiR **tee**-geR), tiger, 20
das **Tigerjunge** (dahs **tee**-geR-yoon-guh), tiger cub, 20
der **Tintenfisch** (daiR **tin**-ten-fish), squid, 22
der **Tisch** (daiR tish), table, 3
die **Tischdecke** (dee **tish**-dek-kuh), tablecloth, 10
das **Tischtennisspiel** (dahs **tish**-ten-nis-shpeel), table tennis, 18
der **Toast** (daiR tohst), toast, 10
der **Toaster** (daiR **toh**-steR), toaster, 3
die **Tochter** (dee **tohK**-teR), daughter, 29
die **Toilette** (dee toy-**let**-tuh), rest rooms, 21; toilet, 2
das **Toilettenpapier** (dahs toy-**let**-ten-pah-peeR), toilet paper, 2
die **Tomaten** (dee toh-**mah**-ten), tomatoes, 6
der **Topf** (daiR tohpf), pot, 24
der **Töpfer** (daiR **tERp**-feR), potter, 24
der **Trabant** (daiR tRah-**bahnt**), satellite, 23
tragen (**tRah**-gen), carry, 27
die **Trainingshosen** (dee **tRai**-nings-hoh-zen), sweatpants, 7
der **Traktor** (daiR **tRahk**-tohR), tractor, 9
der **Transport** (daiR tRahns-**pohRt**), transportation, 16
das **Trapez** (dahs tRah-**payts**), trapeze, 21
der **Trapezkünstler** (daiR tRah-**payts**-kUnst-leR), trapeze artist, 21
die **Trauben** (dee **tRow**-ben), grapes, 6
traurig (**tRow**-RiH), sad, 26
die **Treppe** (dee **tRep**-puh), stairs, 2
der **Tresor** (daiR tRay-**zohR**), safe, 13
das **Trikot** (dahs **tRee**-koht), leotard, 19
trinken (**tRin**-ken), drink, 27
der **Trinkhalm** (daiR **tRink**-hahlm), straw, 10
trocken (**tRohk**-ken), dry, 26
die **Trockenhaube** (dee **tRohk**-ken-how-buh), hair dryer, 12
der **Trockner** (daiR **tRohk**-neR), clothes dryer, 3
die **Trommel** (dee **tRohm**-mel), drum, 19
die **Trompete** (dee tRohm-**pay**-tuh), trumpet, 19
die **Trophäe** (dee tRoh-**fay**), trophy, 18
die **Tuba** (dee **too**-bah), tuba, 19
das **Tuch** (dahs tooK), cloth, 24
die **Tundra** (dee **toon**-dRah), tundra, 32
die **Tür** (dee tUR), door, 2
der **Turban** (daiR tooR-**bahn**), turban, 21
der **Türgriff** (daiR **tUR**-gRif), door handle, 14
der **Turm** (daiR tooRm), tower, 25
die **Turnschuhe** (dee **tooRn**-shoo-uh), gym shoes, 7
die **Tüte** (dee **tU**-tuh), shopping bag, 6

über (**U**-beR), above, 26
die **Überwachungsanlage** (dee **U**-beR-vah-Koongs-ahn-lah-guh), security camera, 13
die **Uhr** (dee ooR), clock, 1; watch, 7
die **Umgebung** (dee **oom**-gay-boong), community, 15
die **Uniform** (dee oo-ni-**fohRm**), uniform, 4
unten (**oon**-ten), down, 26
unter (**oon**-teR), under, 26
das **Unterhemd** (dahs **oon**-teR-hemt), T-shirt, 7
die **Unterschrift** (dee **oon**-teR-shRift), signature, 13

das **Unterseeboot** (dahs **oon**-teR-zay-boht), submarine, 22
die **Unterseite** (dee **oon**-teR-zigh-tuh), bottom, 26
der **Untersuchungstisch** (daiR **oon**-teR-zoo-Koongs-tish), examining table, 11
die **Untertasse** (dee **oon**-teR-tahs-suh), saucer, 10
die **Unterwäsche** (dee **oon**-teR-vay-shuh), underwear, 7
unterwegs (**oon**-teR-vays), going places, 16

die **Vase** (dee **vah**-zuh), vase, 2
der **Vater** (daiR **fah**-teR), father, 29
der **Vati** (daiR **fah**-tee), dad, 29
der **Ventilator** (dair ven-tee-**lah**-tohR), fan, 5
die **Veranda** (dee ve-**Rahn**-dah), deck, 5
verkaufen (faiR-**kow**-fen), sell, 27
der **Verkäufer** (daiR faiR-**koy**-feR), salesman, 15
die **Verkäuferin** (dee faiR-**koy**-fe-Rin), saleswoman, 15
die **Verkehrsampeln** (dee faiR-**kaiR**-sahm-peln), traffic lights, 8, 16
der **Verkehrsstau** (daiR faiR-**kaiRs**-shtow), traffic jam, 8
die **Verwerfung** (dee faiR-**vaiR**-foong), fault, 32
die **Videokamera** (dee **vee**-day-oh-kah-me-Rah), video camera, 17
der **Videorecorder** (daiR **vee**-day-oh-Ray-kohR-deR), videocassette player, 2
vier (feeR), four, 5, 31
das **Viereck** (dahs **FeeR**-ek), square, 30
viert- (feeRt), fourth, 31
vierundachtzig (feeR-oont-**ahKt**-tsiH), eighty-four, 31
vierunddreißig (feeR-oont-**dRigh**-siK), thirty-four, 31
vierundfünfzig (feeR-oont-**fUnf**-tsiH), fifty-four, 31
vierundneunzig (feeR-oont-**noyn**-tsiH), ninety-four, 31
vierundsechzig (feeR-oont-**zeK**-tsiH), sixty-four, 31
vierundsiebzig (feeR-oont-**zeep**-tsiH), seventy-four, 31
vierundvierzig (feeR-oont-**feeR**-tsiH), forty-four, 31
vierundzwanzig (feeR-oont-**tsvahn**-tsiH), twenty-four, 31
vierzehn (**feeR**-tsayhn), fourteen, 31
vierzig (**feeR**-tsiH), forty, 31
der **Vogel** (daiR **foh**-gel), bird, 5
das **Vogelnest** (dahs **foh**-gel-nest), bird's nest, 5
voll (fohl), full, 26
das **Volleyballspiel** (dahs **voh**-lay-bahl-shpeel), volleyball, 18
vor (fohR), in front of, 26
der **Vorhang** (daiR **fohR**-hahng), curtain, 19
die **Vorhänge** (dee **fohR**-hayn-guh), curtains, 2
der **Vulkan** (daiR vool-**kahn**), volcano, 32

die **Waage** (dee **vah**-guh), scale, 6, 13
die **Wache** (dee **vah**-Kuh), security guard, 13
der **Wagenheber** (daiR **vah**-gen-hay-beR), jack, 14
der **Wal** (daiR vahl), whale, 22
der **Wald** (daiR vahlt), forest, 25
das **Waldhorn** (dahs **vahlt**-hohRn), French horn, 19
das **Walroß** (dahs **vahl**-Rohs), walrus, 20
die **Wand** (dee vahnt), wall, 2

English-German Glossary and Index

above, über, 26
accordion, das Akkordeon, 19
acrobat, der Artist, 21
action words, die Tätigkeitswörter, 27
actor, der Schauspieler, 19
actress, die Schauspielerin, 19
address, die Adresse, 13
adjectives, die Adjektive, 26
Africa, Afrika, 32
air hose, der Luftschlauch, 14
air-traffic controller, die
    Luftverkehrskontrolleurin, 17
airplane, das Flugzeug, 16, 17
airport, der Flughafen, 17
alarm clock, der Wecker, 2
alien, der Fremdling, 23
alligator, der Alligator, 20
alphabet, das Alphabet, 1
ambulance, der Krankenwagen, 16
anchor, der Anker, 22
angelfish, der Engelfisch, 22
animals, die Tiere, 20
ankle, der Enkel, 11
ant, die Ameise, 9
Antarctica, Antarktis, 32
antenna, die Antenne, 23
anvil, der Amboß, 25
apartment building, das Wohnhaus, 8
apple, der Apfel, 6
apron, die Schürze, 3
aquarium, das Aquarium, 1
archer, der Bogenschütze, 25
architect, die Architektin, 15
Arctic Ocean, das nördliche Eismeer, 32
arithmetic problem, die Rechenaufgabe, 1
arm, der Arm, 11
armchair, der Sessel, 2
armor, die Rüstung, 25
arrow, der Pfeil, 25
arrowhead, die Pfeilspitze, 24
artist, die Künstlerin, 15
Asia, Asien, 32
asteroid, der Asteroid, 23
astronaut, der Astronaut, 23
astronomer, der Astronom, 15
athlete, der Sportler, 15
Atlantic Ocean, der Atlantik, 32
attic, die Dachstube, 4
audience, die Zuhörer, 19
auditorium, die Aula, 19
aunt, die Tante, 29
Australia, Australien, 32
automatic teller, der Geldautomat, 13
avocado, die Avokado, 6
ax, das Beil, 25

baby, das Baby, 9
baby carriage, der Kinderwagen, 16
back, der Rücken, 11
backpack, der Rucksack, 7
backseat, der Rücksitz, 14
bad, böse, 26
badminton, das Federballspiel, 18
baggage cart, der Gepäckkarren, 17
baggage check-in, die Gepäckabfertigung, 17
baggage claim, die Gepäckausgabe, 17
baggage handler, der Gepäckträger, 17
bakery, die Bäckerei, 8
balcony, der Balkon, 8
bald, kahl, 12
ball gown, das Ballkleid, 4
ballet slippers, die Ballettschuhe, 19
balloon, der Luftballon, 21
banana, die Banane, 6
band, das Orchester, 21
bandage, das Pflaster, 11
bangs, der Pony, 12
bank, die Bank, 13

banker, die Bankbeamtin, 15
banner, das Banner, 25
barbecue, der Grill, 5
barber, der Herrenfriseur, 12
barber shop, beim Herrenfriseur, 12
bareback rider, die sattellose Reiterin, 21
barn, die Scheune, 9
barnacle, die Entenmusche, 22
barrette, die Haarspange, 12
baseball, der Baseball, 18
baseball game, das Baseballspiel, 18
basket, der Korb, 24
basketball, das Korbballspiel, 18
bat (baseball), der Baseballschläger, 18; (animal),
    die Fledermaus, 25
bathing suit, der Badeanzug, 7
bathrobe, der Bademantel, 7
bathroom, das Badezimmer, 2
bathtub, die Badewanne, 2
baton, der Stab, 21
bay, die Bucht, 32
beach, der Strand, 8
beak, der Schnabel, 20
beaker, das Becherglas, 23
bear, der Bär, 20
bear cub, das Bärchen, 20
beard, der Bart, 12
beauty salon, beim Damenfriseur, 12
bed, das Bett, 2
bedroom, das Schlafzimmer, 2
bees, die Bienen, 9
behind, hinter, 26
bell, die Glocke, 1
belt, der Gürtel, 7
bench, die Bank, 8
between, zwischen, 26
bicycle, das Fahrrad, 14, 16, 18
bicycle chain, die Fahrradkette, 14
big top, das Zirkuszelt, 21
bill, der Schein, 13
billion, die Milliarde, 31
binoculars, das Fernglas, 17
bird, der Vogel, 5
bird's nest, das Vogelnest, 5
birthday party, die Geburtstagsfeier, 10
bison, der Bison, 24
black, schwarz, 12, 28
blacksmith, der Hufschmied, 25
blanket, die Decke, 2
blimp, das Luftschiff, 16
blocks, die Bauklötze, 4
blond, blond, 12
blood, das Blut, 11
blouse, die Bluse, 7
blow dryer, der Fön, 12
blue, blau, 28
board, das Brett, 3
boat, das Boot, 16
bone, der Knochen, 24
book, das Buch, 1
bookcase, das Bücherregal, 1
bookseller, der Buchhändler, 15
bookstore, die Buchhandlung, 8
boots, die Stiefel, 7
bottle, die Flasche, 6
bottom, die Unterseite, 26
boulder, der Felsblock, 24
bow (knot), die Schleife, 13; (violin), der Bogen,
    19; (weapon), der Bogen, 25
bowl, die Schüssel, 10
bowling, das Kegeln, 18
box, die Schachtel, 4
boxing, das Boxen, 18
boxing gloves, die Boxhandschuhe, 18
boy, der Junge, 9
bracelet, das Armband, 7
braces, die Klammern, 11
braid, der Zopf, 12
brake lights, die Bremslichter, 14

branch, der Zweig, 5
bread, das Brot, 6
break, brechen, 27
breakfast, das Frühstück, 10
brick, der Backstein, 3
bridge, die Brücke, 16
briefcase, die Aktentasche, 17
broccoli, der Brokkoli, 10
broom, der Besen, 3
brother, der Bruder, 29
brown, braun, 12, 28
brush, die Bürste, 12
bubble, die Blase, 22
bucket, der Eimer, 24
buckle, die Schnalle, 7
building, das Gebäude, 8
bull, der Bulle, 9
bulletin board, die Anzeigetafel, 1
bun, der Knoten, 12
buoy, die Boje, 22
bus, der Bus, 16
bus driver, die Busfahrerin, 15
bus stop, die Bushaltestelle, 16
bush, der Busch, 5
butcher, der Metzger, 15
butcher shop, die Metzgerei, 8
butter, die Butter, 6
butterfly, der Schmetterling, 5
button, der Knopf, 7
buy, kaufen, 27

cabbage, das Kraut, 6
cactus, der Kaktus, 1
cage, der Käfig, 21
cake, der Kuchen, 10
calculator, der Rechner, 1
calendar, der Kalender, 1
calf, das Kalb, 9
camel, das Kamel, 20
camera, die Kamera, 17, 21
camper, der Wohnwagen, 16
can, die Dose, 6
canal, der Kanal, 32
candle, die Kerze, 10
candy, die Süßigkeiten, 6
cane, der Stock, 11
cannon, die Kanone, 22
canoe, das Kanu, 16
cap, die Strickmütze, 7
cape (clothing), das Cape, 21; (geography), das
    Kap, 32
car, das Auto, 16
car racing, das Autorennen, 18
car wash, die Autowaschanlage, 14
caramel apple, der kandierte Apfel, 21
cardinal numbers, die Grundzahlen, 31
cards, die Karten, 4
cargo bay, der Frachtraum, 23
carpenter, der Schreiner, 15
carpet, der Teppich, 2
carrots, die Karotten, 6
carry, tragen, 27
cart, der Karren, 24
cartwheel, das Rad, 21
cash register, die Kasse, 6
cashier, die Kassiererin, 6
cassette player, der Kassettenrecorder, 2
cassette tape, die Kassette, 2
cast, der Gipsverband, 11
castle, das Schloß, 25
cat, die Katze, 9
catch, fangen, 27
cave, die Höhle, 24
cave drawing, die Höhlenmalerei, 24
cave dwellers, die Höhlenbewohner, 24
ceiling, die Decke, 2
celery, der Sellerie, 10
cello, das Cello, 19

cellophane tape, der Tesafilm, 1
cement mixer, der Zementmixer, 16
cereal, die Cornflakes, 6
chain mail, das Kettenhemd, 25
chair, der Stuhl, 3
chalk, die Kreide, 1
chalkboard, die Wandtafel, 1
channel, die Meerenge, 32
check, der Scheck, 13
checkbook, das Scheckbuch, 13
checkers, das Mühlespiel, 4
cheek, die Wange, 11
cheese, der Käse, 6
cherries, die Kirsche, 6
chess, das Schachspiel, 4
chest, die Brust, 11
chick, das Hühnchen, 9
chicken, das Hühnerfleisch, 10
children, die Kinder, 19
chimney, der Kamin, 2
chin, das Kinn, 11
chocolate, die Schokolade, 6
church, die Kirche, 8
circle, der Kreis, 30
circus, der Zirkus, 21
circus parade, die Zirkusparade, 21
city, die Stadt, 8
clam, die Muschel, 22
clarinet, die Klarinette, 19
classroom, das Klassenzimmer, 1
claws, die Krallen, 20
clay, der Lehm, 24
clean, sauber, 26
climb, klettern, 27
clock, die Uhr, 1
close, zumachen, 27
closed, zu, 26
closet, der Wandschrank, 2
cloth, das Tuch, 24
clothes dryer, der Trockner, 3
clothing, die Kleidung, 7
clothing store, der Bekleidungsladen, 8
clouds, die Wolken, 5
clown, der Clown, 21
club, die Keule, 24
coat, der Mantel, 7
cobweb, die Spinnwebe, 4
coffee, der Kaffee, 10
coin, die Münze, 13
cold, kalt, 26
collar, der Kragen, 7
colored pencils, die Farbstifte, 1
coloring book, das Malbuch, 4
colors, die Farben, 28
colt, das Fohlen, 9
comb, der Kamm, 12
come, kommen, 27
comet, der Komet, 23
comic books, die Comics, 4
community, die Umgebung, 15
compact disc, die Compact Disc, 2
compass (magnetic), der Kompaß, 32; (drawing), der Zirkel, 1
computer, der Komputer, 23
computer programmer, die Komputerprogrammiererin, 15
Concorde, die Concorde, 17
conductor, der Dirigent, 19
cone, der Kegel, 30
constellation, das Sternbild, 23
construction worker, der Bauarbeiter, 15
control panel, die Kontrolltafel, 23
control tower, der Kontrollturm, 17
cook (noun), der Koch, 15; (verb), kochen, 27
cookies, die Plätzchen, 6
copilot, der Kopilot, 17
coral, die Koralle, 22
coral reef, das Korallenriff, 22
corn, der Mais, 24
corner, die Ecke, 8
costume, das Kostüm, 19
cotton candy, die Zuckerwatte, 21
counter, die Theke, 3

country, das Land, 9
court jester, der Hofnarr, 25
courtyard, der Hof, 25
cousin (female), die Kusine, 29; (male), der Cousin, 29
coveralls, der Overall, 14
cow, die Kuh, 9
cowboy, der Cowboy, 15
cowboy boots, die Cowboystiefel, 4
cowboy hat, der Cowboyhut, 4
crab, die Krabbe, 22
crackers, die Kekse, 6
cradle, die Wiege, 4
crane, der Kran, 8
crater, der Krater, 23
crayon, der Buntstift, 1
cream, die Sahne, 10
credit card, die Kreditkarte, 13
crew cut, der amerikanische Haarschnitt, 12
crop, die Ernte, 24
cross-country skiing, der Langlauf, 18
crosswalk, der Fußgängerübergang, 16
crown, die Krone, 25
cruise ship, der Passagierdampfer, 16
crutch, die Krücke, 11
cry, weinen, 27
cube, der Würfel, 30
cup, die Tasse, 10
curlers, die Lockenwickel, 12
curling iron, der Lockenstab, 12
curly, lockig, 12
curtain, der Vorhang, 19
curtains, die Vorhänge, 2
customs officer, die Zollbeamtin, 17
cut, schneiden, 27
cycling, das Radfahren, 18
cylinder, der Zylinder, 30
cymbals, die Becken, 19

dad, der Vati, 29
dance, tanzen, 27
dancer, die Tänzerin, 19
dark, dunkel, 26
dashboard, das Armaturenbrett, 14
daughter, die Tochter, 29
deck, die Veranda, 5
deer, das Reh, 20
dental floss, der Zahnfaden, 11
dental hygienist, die Zahnassistentin, 11
dentist, der Zahnarzt, 11
dentist's office, beim Zahnarzt, 11
desert, die Wüste, 32
desk (pupil's), das Pult, 1; (teacher's), das Lehrerpult, 1
dice, die Würfel, 4
difficult, schwierig, 26
dig, graben, 27
dining room, das Eßzimmer, 2
dinner, das Abendessen, 10
dinosaur, der Dinosaurier, 24
dirt, der Schmutz, 9
dirty, schmutzig, 26
disc jockey, der Discjockey, 15
dishes, das Geschirr, 3
dishwasher, die Spülmaschine, 3
dive, tauchen, 27
diving, das Tauchen, 18
dock, der Pier, 16
doctor, die Ärztin, 11
doctor's office, beim Arzt, 11
dog, der Hund, 9
doll, die Puppe, 4
dollhouse, das Puppenhaus, 4
dolphin, der Delphin, 22
donkey, der Esel, 9
door, die Tür, 2
door handle, der Türgriff, 14
doorman, der Portier, 15
down, unten, 26
down vest, die Daunenweste, 7
downhill skiing, der Abfahrtslauf, 18
dragon, der Drache, 25

draw, zeichnen, 27
drawbridge, die Zugbrücke, 25
drawer, die Schublade, 3
dress, das Kleid, 7
dresser, die Frisierkommode, 2
dressing room, das Ankleidezimmer, 19
drill, der Bohrer, 3
drink, trinken, 27
drive, fahren, 27
drive-in, der Autoschalter, 13
driver's seat, der Fahrersitz, 14
driveway, die Auffahrt, 8
drugstore, die Apotheke, 8
drum, die Trommel, 19
dry, trocken, 26
duck, die Ente, 9
duckling, das Entchen, 9
dull, stumpf, 26
dungeon, der Kerker, 25
dust, der Staub, 4
dustpan, die Kehrichtschaufel, 3

eagle, der Adler, 20
ear, das Ohr, 11
earmuffs, die Ohrenschützer, 7
earring, der Ohrring, 7
Earth, die Erde, 23
easel, die Staffelei, 1
east, der Osten, 32
easy, einfach, 26
eat, essen, 27
eggs, die Eier, 6
eight, acht, 31
eighteen, achtzehn, 31
eighth, acht-, 31
eighty, achtzig, 31
eighty-eight, achtundachtzig, 31
eighty-five, fünfundachtzig, 31
eighty-four, vierundachtzig, 31
eighty-nine, neunundachtzig, 31
eighty-one, einundachtzig, 31
eighty-seven, siebenundachtzig, 31
eighty-six, sechsundachtzig, 31
eighty-three, dreiundachtzig, 31
eighty-two, zweiundachtzig, 31
elbow, der Ellbogen, 11
electric mixer, der Mixer, 3
electric train, der elektrische Zug, 4
electrical outlet, die Steckdose, 3
electrician, der Elektriker, 15
elephant, der Elefant, 20, 21
elevator, der Aufzug, 17
eleven, elf, 31
elf, der Elf, 25
empty, leer, 26
engine, der Motor, 14, 17
equator, der Äquator, 32
eraser (chalkboard), der Schwamm, 1; (pencil), der Radiergummi, 1
escalator, die Rolltreppe, 17
Europe, Europa, 32
examining table, der Untersuchungstisch, 11
eyebrow, die Augenbraue, 11
eyes, die Augen, 11

face, das Gesicht, 11
factory, die Fabrik, 8
factory worker, die Fabrikarbeiterin, 15
fairy, die Fee, 25
fall (season), der Herbst, 5
fall (verb), fallen, 27
family tree, der Stammbaum, 29
fan (electric), der Ventilator, 5; (hand), der Fächer, 4
far, fern, 26
farm, der Bauernhof, 9
farmer, der Bauer, 9
fashion designer, die Modeschöpferin, 15
fast, schnell, 26
fat, dick, 26
father, der Vater, 29

faucet, der Wasserhahn, 3
fault, die Verwerfung, 32
feather, die Feder, 4
feathers, die Federn, 20
fence, der Zaun, 9
fender, der Kotflügel, 14
fern, der Farn, 24
field, das Feld, 24
fifteen, fünfzehn, 31
fifth, fünft-, 31
fifty, fünfzig, 31
fifty-eight, achtundfünfzig, 31
fifty-five, fünfundfünfzig, 31
fifty-four, vierundfünfzig, 31
fifty-nine, neunundfünfzig, 31
fifty-one, einundfünfzig, 31
fifty-seven, siebenundfünfzig, 31
fifty-six, sechsundfünfzig, 31
fifty-three, dreiundfünfzig, 31
fifty-two, zweiundfünfzig, 31
file, der Feile, 3
file cabinet, der Aktenschrank, 13
film, der Film, 21
fin, die Flosse, 22
find, finden, 27
finger, der Finger, 11
fingernail, der Fingernagel, 12
fire, das Feuer, 24
fire engine, das Feuerwehrauto, 16
fire escape, die Rettungsleiter, 8
fire fighter, der Feuerwehrmann, 15
fire hydrant, der Hydrant, 8
fire station, die Feuerwehrzentrale, 8
fireplace, der Kamin, 2
first, erst-, 31
fish, der Fisch, 1, 10
fisherman, der Fischer, 15
fishhook, der Angelhaken, 22
fishing, das Fischen, 24
fishing line, die Angelschnur, 22
five, fünf, 31
fix, reparieren, 27
flags, die Fahnen, 17
flamingo, der Flamingo, 20
flashbulb, das Blitzlicht, 21
flashlight, die Taschenlampe, 3
flat tire, die Panne, 14
flight attendant, der Flugbegleiter, 17
flint, der Feuerstein, 24
flipper, die Schwimmflosse, 22
floor, der Fußboden, 2
florist, die Blumenhändlerin, 15
flour, das Mehl, 3
flowerbed, das Blumenbeet, 5
flowers, die Blumen, 5
flute, die Flöte, 19
fly (insect), die Fliege, 5
fly (verb), fliegen, 27
fly swatter, die Fliegenklatsche, 5
fog, der Nebel, 5
food, das Essen, 6
food processor, die Küchenmaschine, 3
foot, der Fuß, 11
football (game), das amerikanische Fußballspiel, 18
footprint, die Fußstapfe, 23
footstool, der Fußbank, 2
forehead, die Stirn, 11
foreman, der Bauleiter, 15
forest, der Wald, 25
forge, die Schmiede, 25
fork, die Gabel, 10
forty, vierzig, 31
forty-eight, achtundvierzig, 31
forty-five, fünfundvierzig, 31
forty-four, vierundvierzig, 31
forty-nine, neunundvierzig, 31
forty-one, einundvierzig, 31
forty-seven, siebenundvierzig, 31
forty-six, sechsundvierzig, 31
forty-three, dreiundvierzig, 31
forty-two, zweiundvierzig, 31
fountain, der Brunnen, 8

four, vier, 5, 31
fourteen, vierzehn, 31
fourth, viert-, 31
fox, der Fuchs, 20
freckles, die Sommersprossen, 12
freezer, die Tiefkühltruhe, 3
french fries, die Pommes frites, 10
French horn, das Waldhorn, 19
frog, der Frosch, 9
frozen dinner, die Tiefkühlkost, 6
fruit, das Obst, 6
fruit juice, der Fruchtsaft, 6
full, voll, 26
fur, der Pelz, 24

galaxy, die Milchstraße, 23
game, das Spiel, 4
garage, die Garage, 14
garden hose, der Gartenschlauch, 5
gardener, der Gärtner, 15
garment bag, der Kleidersack, 17
gas cap, der Tankverschluß, 14
gas pump, die Zapfsäule, 14
gas station, die Tankstelle, 14
gate, der Flugsteig, 17
giant, der Riese, 25
gift, das Geschenk, 10
gills, die Kiemen, 22
giraffe, die Giraffe, 20
girl, das Mädchen, 9
give, geben, 27
glacier, der Gletscher, 32
glass, das Glas, 10
glasses, die Brille, 7
globe, der Globus, 1
gloves, die Handschuhe, 7
glue, der Klebstoff, 1
Go!, Geh!, 16
go, gehen, 27
goat, die Zeige, 9
goggles, die Schutzbrille, 18
going places, Unterwegs, 16
gold (metal), das Gold, 22; (color), golden, 28
golf, das Golfspiel, 18
golf club, der Golfschläger, 18
good, gut, 26
goose, die Gans, 9
gorilla, der Gorilla, 20
gosling, das Gänslein, 9
grandfather, der Großvater, 29
grandma, die Oma, 29
grandmother, die Großmutter, 29
grandpa, der Opa, 29
grapefruit, die Pampelmuse, 6
grapes, die Trauben, 6
grass, das Gras, 9
grasshopper, die Heuschrecke, 5
gray, grau, 28
green, grün, 28
green beans, die grünen Bohnen, 6
grocery store, das Lebensmittelgeschäft, 8
guitar, die Guitarre, 19
gulf, der Golf, 32
gym shoes, die Turnschuhe, 7
gymnastics, das Geräteturnen, 18

hair, die Haare, 12
hair dryer, die Trockenhaube, 12
hair spray, der Haarfestiger, 12
hairstylist, die Friseuse, 12
half, halb, 31
ham, der Schinken, 10
hamburger, der Hamburger, 10
hammer, der Hammer, 3
hammock, die Hängematte, 5
hand (clock), der Zeiger, 1; (person), die Hand, 11
hand brake, die Handbremse, 14
handkerchief, das Taschentuch, 7
handlebars, die Lenkstange, 14
handstand, der Handstand, 21

hang glider, der Drachenflieger, 16
hangar, die Flugzeughalle, 17
hanger, der Kleiderbügel, 2
happy, glücklich, 26
hard, hart, 26
harp, die Harfe, 19
hat, der Hut, 4, 7
hay, das Heu, 9
head, der Kopf, 11
headlight, der Scheinwerfer, 14
headset, der Kopfhörer, 17
headstand, der Kopfstand, 21
heavy, schwer, 26
helicopter, der Hubschrauber, 16
helm, der Helm, 22
helmet, der Helm, 18
hen, das Huhn, 9
high jump, der Hochsprung, 18
hiking boots, die Wanderstiefel, 7
hill, der Hügel, 9
hippopotamus, das Flußpferd, 20
history, die Geschichte, 24
hockey, das Hockey, 18
hole punch, der Locher, 1
hood (clothing), die Kapuze, 7; (car), die Schutzhaube, 14
hoof, der Huf, 20
hoop, der Reifen, 21
horns, die Hörner, 9, 20
horse, das Pferd, 9
horse racing, das Pferderennen, 18
horseback riding, das Reiten, 18
horseshoe, das Hufeisen, 25
hospital, das Krankenhaus, 8
hot, heiß, 26
hot-air balloon, der Ballon, 16
hotel, das Hotel, 8
house, das Haus, 2
hubcap, die Nabe, 14
human history, die Menschheitsgeschichte, 24
hump, der Höcker, 20
hundred, hundert, 31
hundred thousand, hundert tausend, 31
hunt, die Jagd, 26
hunter, der Jäger, 24
hurdles, das Hürdenrennen, 18
hut, die Hütte, 24
hypodermic needle, die Spritze, 11

ice, das Eis, 5
ice cream, das Eis, 10
ice cubes, die Eiswürfel, 3
iceberg, der Eisberg, 32
icecap, die Eiskappe, 32
icicle, der Eiszapfen, 5
in front of, vor, 26
Indian Ocean, der Indische Ozean, 32
ink pad, das Stempelkissen, 13
insect, das Insekt, 24
inside, innerhalb, 26
intersection, die Straßenkreuzung, 16
iron, das Bügeleisen, 3
ironing board, das Bügelbrett, 3
island, die Insel, 32

jack, der Wagenheber, 14
jacket, die Jacke, 7
jaguar, der Jaguar, 20
jail, das Gefängnis, 8
jam, die Konfitüre, 10
jeans, die Jeans, 7
jeep, der Jeep, 16
jellyfish, die Qualle, 22
jewel, das Juwel, 22
jeweler, der Juwelier, 15
jigsaw puzzle, das Puzzle, 4
jogging, das Joggen, 18
judge, die Richterin, 15
juggle, jonglieren, 27
juggler, der Jongleur, 21
jump, springen, 27